Other Books By Tian Dayton

Drama Games
Techniques For Self-Development

Daily Affirmations
For Parents

Sept– 07

*to the Murrays, who
work on marriage —
what a concept ♡*

Daily Affirmations For

Forgiving
And
Moving On

God Bless,

Tian Dayton, M.A., A.M.S.

*your St. Francis
family.*

Health Communications, Inc.
Deerfield Beach, Florida

Tian Dayton, M.A., A.M.S.
Innerlook, Inc.
262 Central Park West
New York, New York 10024

©1992 Tian Dayton
ISBN 1-55874-215-8

Publisher: Health Communications, Inc.
          3201 S.W. 15th Street
          Deerfield Beach, FL 33442-8190

Cover design by Robert Cannata

*D*edication

I remember having an argument on my Grandmother's front stairs with my cousin when I was about five. He insisted that our grandmother was his alone. I, being the older, tried to explain to him that she really belonged to both of us. But, upon reflection, this is her magic. That somehow she has given each of us the feeling that she is our own private "Grammie," belonging to each of us in a very special way.

I would like to dedicate this book to you, Grammie. Thank you for your steadiness, faith and love. It has embodied *forgiving* and *moving* on for all of us.

Acknowledgments

I would like to extend my appreciation to Marie Stilkind for feeling the importance of this subject and supporting its publication. Many thanks to Marie Stilkind and Diane Zarowin for their skillful and conscientious editing. Thanks go to Dr. Benny Pascario for always being there in such important ways. Much love to my family of origin and extended family for being in some deep sense a part of all the pages in this book. Great fondness and gratitude to my friends, to the 12-Step program and to my wonderful clients and students. Lastly, thank you always to my husband, Brandt, and our children, Marina and Alex, just for being them and letting me be me.

People say that what we're all seeking is a meaning for life . . . I don't think that's what we're really seeking. I think what we're seeking is an experience of being alive so that the life experiences that we have on a purely physical plane will have resonances within that are those of our innermost being . . .

We're so engaged in doing things to achieve purposes of outer value that we forget that it's the inner value that is the rapture associated with being alive that it's all about . . .

The ultimate mystery of being is beyond all mystery of thought.

Joseph Campbell

*I*ntroduction

There is a point in recovery when we seem to stand in the center of our own decision about who we are and how we want to be. It comes after enough of the past pain, resentment and grief has been spent, enough deep holes and yearnings have been filled, enough baggage from the past dealt with to restore ourselves to a "good enough" status, ready to meet life more or less as it is happening.

At this point we need to recognize which attitudes and behavior patterns will serve us throughout the rest of our lives and which need to be let go of. Can the lives we have envisioned for ourselves in recovery flourish under the weight of carried resentment from the past? What does it cost us in terms of happiness and well-being to hang on to blame and hurt?

We cannot do a flying leap over pain and resentment to forgiveness without first working through those feelings and restoring our lost sense of self. Similarly, we cannot step over forgiveness and truly be in full possession of our selves and our happiness. Forgiveness and letting go are part of our road to happiness. Our road to health could be broken down into these steps:

1. Recognizing a need to change.
2. Reaching out for help toward people or a Higher Power.
3. Allowing past pain, anger, resentment and grief to come to the surface and be felt in the present.
4. Identifying developmental gaps and rebuilding a self.
5. Sharing these feelings with others, gaining and giving support, acceptance and nurturing.
6. Accepting our selves and our lives as they are.
7. Forgiving and letting go of or making peace with the past.
8. Restoring trust in self, relationships, life and a Higher Power.
9. Becoming willing or able to live life one day at a time in the present.

Forgiveness and letting go are steps on our road back to health and happiness. Without them we will never be free of our pasts. We deserve to move on. We need not be held hostage to our pasts if we are willing to release and grow beyond them.

Only we can ultimately free ourselves. No one can do this for us. *Forgiving And Moving On* is a book of daily affirmations to assist in this process and a sharing of experience, strength and hope along the way.

Believing In Inner Healing

*T*oday I will do my part to follow through on an inner change. When something inside of me has truly been worked through and released, I will believe in it. I have been restored to sanity. It is in my ability to believe in this that will make it real in my day-to-day life. When I refuse to really accept that an inner transformation has taken place, I sabotage my own getting well — I take away the inner healing by telling myself that it is not real. I have the courage today to believe that a Higher Power is at work in my life and that I am meant to be whole and happy.

I have the courage to heal.

Work and love — these are the basics;
Waking life is a dream controlled.

George Santayana

Forgiveness

Today I understand the true meaning of forgiveness. I had thought that forgiving was what good and nice people did. I thought I should do it because it was the right thing to do. I now understand that to forgive someone else is to forgive myself. When I hold anger in my mind, my unconscious does not know for whom that feeling is meant — it only knows that it is a container for resentment. To forgive is to let go and to release my own mind from being caught in the cycle of going over and over the hurt. I am not forgiving for the good of the other person. I am forgiving for the good of myself so that I can be free and move on. Forgiveness is a gift, a state of grace that benefits the giver as much as or more than the receiver. If I am to heal fully, I will need to forgive fully.

I forgive for my own sake.

Do as the heavens have done, forget your evil;
With them forgive yourself.
                                    William Shakespeare

Feeling Anger

When I feel angry, I seem to have two ways of dealing with it. I either hold it in and say nothing or I let it out in accusing, venting, nonproductive ways. When I do this, I rupture perfectly good relationships. It is fair for me to register disgruntled feelings when appropriate but that's all I need to do. When I can't hold back from getting into an argument using blame and accusation, I create a mess. When something goes wrong, feeling angry is normal. I need to give myself a few minutes to feel the anger before I act out the feeling, rather than immediately dumping it on someone else. When I can give myself permission to feel my own anger without fearing it will devour me, I can own it as mine and decide what to do with it next.

It is okay to feel anger.
It is okay to let anger go.

Remember, you can't steal second if you don't take your foot off first.

Mike Todd

Intimate Relationships

I can have intimate relationships in my life today. In the past I felt abandoned by those nearest to me and as a result, it is difficult for me to trust. I am strong enough now to weather the feelings that come up for me as I move close to another human being because I can feel my own feelings and give voice to them. I can simply see them without creating a problem by blaming them on someone else. They are my feelings and I am willing to own them. I can be close to someone.

I can tolerate the feelings that come with intimacy.

Much of your pain is self-chosen.
It is the bitter potion by which the physician within you heals your sick self. Therefore, trust the physician, and drink his remedy in silence and tranquility: For his hand, though heavy and hard, is guided by the tender hand of the Unseen.

Kahlil Gibran

Healthy Dependence

There is a vast difference between healthy dependence and co-dependence. In healthy dependence I feel my own feelings, own them and share them openly with someone else, and I allow that person to do the same with me. In co-dependence, I become lodged within another person's psyche and feel their feelings for them, losing touch with what I am feeling. Today I understand that it is healthy to have comfortable interdependent relationships where all members take responsibility for themselves and their own thoughts and feelings. I can lean on someone without falling over because my center of gravity is within me.

I can have intimacy in my life.

———

Never idealize others.
They will never live up to your expectations.
Don't over-analyze your relationships.
Stop playing games. A growing relationship
can only be nurtured by genuineness.

Leo Buscaglia

Self-Care

Today I will be gentle with myself. Only I know how hurt I have been and how frightened I am capable of being. I will hold that terror-stricken part of me with loving, kind hands and ask for help from a higher, wiser source. I will stand as the caretaker of my own soul and protect it. I will take risks by not pretending to myself or others that I am fearless or by playing tough and hiding underneath layers of denial. If I am to invite my spirit to live freely within me, I will need to be both loving and strong — strong enough to live with my own weakness and loving enough to extend a compassionate hand to myself when I need it. I accept and love myself not as I think I should be but as I am.

I will treat myself with gentle respect.

———

*Out of suffering have emerged
the strongest souls; the most massive
characters are seared with scars.*

E. H. Chapin

Dysfunctional Pasts

Dysfunctional pasts are tricky, sticky things to disentangle from. Because I felt unseen and isolated in my family, much of my sense of being close came through conflict and entanglement. We really didn't know how to spend time together in a relaxed way. We were all on constant guard. Today I recognize that I reach for chaos and conflict the way an alcoholic reaches for a drink. I unconsciously wait for trouble to start, then I protect myself against the agony of anticipation by producing it in the form of either actual contention or a kind of hysterical fun that is also based in tension and fear. Today I recognize this for what it is and see it all in a sympathetic light.

I forgive myself for participating
in this dynamic and understand that
I couldn't help it.

———

A great many people think they are think-
ing when they are merely rearranging their
prejudices.

William James

Blaming Others

Today I understand that dumping blame on someone else does not relieve pain or make my life better in any way. If I reach out to others by attacking and blaming them, how can I expect them to hear anything that I say. If I want to be heard, I need to risk being seen — not as I wish to be seen but as I am. I ask too much of someone else when I say obnoxious things and yet insist on being heard. If I really want someone to understand me, I need to risk being vulnerable and let my feelings show. Pointing a finger at someone else will only make them want to point a finger at me. It is hard to feel vulnerable, but with practice, it will become easier. I will be left with more of my real self if I do not tear at the self of someone else.

I take this small step toward great growth.

Begin to weave and God will
give you the thread.

German proverb

Today I know the truth of my recovery. If I am to stand centered and strong within my life and self, I will need to plant a garden within my own soul. A garden for me to nurture and to nurture me. A haven of beauty. I will find my own voice and sing my song because if I don't sing it, it will not be sung. It is all I have and it is enough. I do not need to prove anything to anyone anymore. I have come home — to me. The truth is I was here all along, only I forgot to look for myself. Instead I searched for me in other people's meaning and became lost in their stories. I am not lost today. I know that there is nowhere to look for me but within myself and no one to lead me there but me. Thank you, life, for letting me see this.

I am home within me.

———

If you would be happy for a week,
take a wife. If you would be happy for a month,
kill a pig. But if you would be happy
all your life, plant a garden.

Ancient Chinese proverb

Looking Backward

Today I am willing to face both my past and my present. If I close my eyes to my past, I am kidding myself — no one has no past. If I live in my past, I am robbing myself because my present will slip by as if it never happened. I am going to find a working balance, one in which I can see day to day how my past has shaped who I am today. If my past is causing me problems, I will find appropriate methods and places to work those out so that I do not pollute my present. I will also remember that my present is important, that working through my past does not mean living in it; it just means that I am willing to re-experience and rework certain parts of it so that I can release it and move on.

I am willing to live with
all of who I am.

The great art of life is knowing how
to turn the surplus life of the
soul into life for the body.
Henry David Thoreau

Trusting The Good Times

Today I am capable of allowing my life to feel good. My habit pattern from my past has taught me that when life is going well, not to trust it. I unconsciously wait for the bottom to fall out when life feels too good, fearing what I learned as a child, that it will not last. When I get like this, I do something to mess things up. Just being aware of this will help me to ride out the good times, as threatening as they may be. It is the nature of life for nothing to last, good or bad. Good and bad are the judgments we bring. Actually life is like a constantly changing kaleidoscopic series of events, presenting themselves over and over again in endless variety. Understanding this makes it easier to step back and enjoy life for what it is. It can give me a stage upon which I enact my play, but it cannot give me meaning. I give life meaning by my attitude toward it.

I will flow with the times.

The person who does not make a choice makes a choice.
                                        Jewish proverb

Stored Anger

Today I am willing to take responsibility for the anger that I carry within me. I am not a bad person because I feel angry. No one wants to think of themselves as an angry person, and I am no exception. But when I refuse to acknowledge the anger and resentment that I have stored within me, (1) I turn my back on me and refuse to accept a very important part of myself and (2) I ask the people close to me to hold my feelings for me, to be the containers of my unconscious or the feelings inside of myself that I do not wish to see. Because I deny my anger to myself does not mean that it goes away. Today I am willing to consider that there might be something more to it, that I may be carrying feelings of anger that I need to accept.

I am willing to experience my own anger.

Let us take men as they are, not as they ought to be.

Franz Schubert

Detaching With Love

Today I understand why detaching with love has been difficult for me. It has taken me a long time to understand truly that there are some things I can do absolutely nothing about. My past taught me to remain in the cycle of fixing and doing. It seemed less painful to be stuck in trying than to let go and risk the pain of loneliness. What I did not know was that in letting go I would feel enormous relief and a renewed sense of energy with which to rebuild those areas of my life that needed attention. Detaching with love is not difficult when I accept my own limitations.

There are some people, things and situations that I can do nothing about.

Keep love in your heart. A life without it is like a sunless garden when the flowers are dead. The consciousness of loving and being loved brings a warmth and richness to life that nothing else can bring.

Oscar Wilde

Growth

Today I let go and become real. I know that by holding on too tightly I squeeze the life out of myself and those around me. Recovery has taught me to value being authentic above being something or someone. Recovery is a process of facing and removing those obstacles that have been in the way on my own road back to myself. It has been my willingness to risk and trust that my Higher Power will hold me that has brought me to life again. Now it is time for me to live each day as it comes and give some of what I have received. So many people have helped me along the way — it is also part of my recovery to share what I have learned in case it might help someone else.

I am open to life and all it holds.

———

To remain whole, be twisted!
To become straight, let yourself be bent.
To become full, be hollow.
Be tattered, that you may be renewed.

Lao-tzu

Today I understand that when I project my feelings outward and see them as belonging to other people and not to me, I postpone my own self-awareness. The only way I can deal with difficult feelings is first to claim them as my own. Sitting with anxiety, anger, rage and jealousy is not pleasant, but actually experiencing my own feelings is the only way to get through them.

*I own my feelings and am willing
to experience them.*

One afternoon, when veteran American League baseball umpire Bill Guthrie was working behind the plate, the catcher for the visiting team repeatedly protested his calls. Guthrie endured this for three innings. In the fourth inning, Guthrie stopped him. "Son," he said gently. "You've been a big help to me in calling the balls and strikes and I appreciate it. But I think I've got the hang of it now. So I'm going to ask you to go to the clubhouse and show whoever's there how to take a shower."

Dan McKinnon

New Ways Of Being

There will be times when I do not feel up to things — when there seems to be too big a gap between who I think I am and who I want to be. I believe in being true to myself and basically honest. When I first try something new, it may feel as if I am trying on an article of clothing that doesn't quite suit me. But there is nothing wrong with acting "as if." I may need to practice new behaviors in order to become comfortable with them. Sometimes when I allow myself to act "as if," the old me sort of falls away and gives room to something new. Children do this all the time, trying on different roles and playing with them. There is no reason to commit myself to a limited view of who I am. I can be who I want to be.

I can practice new ways of being.

———

All that we see or seem is but a dream within a dream.

Edgar Allen Poe

Seeing A Situation Differently

Today I will attempt to see anything I am involved with from more than one perspective. If I feel myself getting stuck in the way I see things, I will say to myself, "I wish to see this differently," and know that my sincere desire will result in a shift of awareness. There is really no one right way to see anything. To allow my point of view to shift will not only produce insight and relief for a particular circumstance but it will give me practice in letting my mind move freely and independently. I will allow myself the luxury of relaxing my rigid point of view and letting new light and fresh awareness come into my inner sight. I believe that it is possible to see things in a variety of ways.

*I sincerely wish to see this
in a different light.*

———

This cannot hide the light I wish to see.
We stand in light.
In the light this will look different.

from *A Course In Miracles*

Creativity And Spontaneity

Today I will cut myself loose a little from the constraints that bind me. If I am going to enjoy my day, I need to enter into it as if it were altogether fresh, with potential adventure waiting around the corner. What happens today has never happened before — I am co-creating my world anew each day, and knowing this unites me with the energy of a Higher Power. We are creating together, living and exploring. I don't know from where I arrived in this world or why but as long as I am here, I will live — I won't waste this day.

I will choose life.

Look, I really don't want to wax philosophic, but I will say that if you're alive, you've got to flap your arms and legs, you've got to jump around a lot, you've got to make a lot of noise, because life is the very opposite of death. And therefore, as I see it, if you're quiet, you're not living . . . you've got to be noisy, or at least your thoughts should be noisy and colorful and lively.

Mel Brooks

I will live the life that I have in front of me today. I get so caught up in what I would like to be, I forget to be what I am. I believe today that there is a plan for me and that my life is unfolding as it is meant to. I remove my energy from myself and my own life when I suspend it in waiting for my real life to finally happen. My real life is happening today. It does not require waiting, organizing or planning. I just need to step into it. If the doors I am beating against are not opening, perhaps there is a good reason for that. Why don't I enjoy strolling through the many doors that are already open to me? My life is here and now, not if and when. It feels good to live in the present.

I will show up for my life today.

You don't get to choose how you're going to die. Or when. You can only decide how you're going to live. Now.

Joan Baez

I Am Meant To Be Happy

I have so much in my life to be grateful for — there is so much that is going well for me — so much that feels right and good. I have worked hard to know a feeling like this and today I will let myself have it. I really believe that the purpose of life is to be happy. In my lack of awareness of myself I have perpetuated an old habit pattern of focusing on the negative. Things can be basically good but if there is one thing going wrong, that is what will take my focus and occupy my attention. It is time for me to accept being happy. At one time in my life I lost happiness, and since then I have never trusted life enough to relax and accept good and grace. I want to trust that my days are meant for me to enjoy as I did when I was a child before I learned differently. I want to trust life as I did when I was young.

I am here to be happy.

Just try to be happy. Unhappiness starts with wanting to be happier.

Sam Levenson

Forgiveness And Freedom

Today I understand that in forgiving someone else I free myself. I held back on forgiveness because it seemed too kind an act for those who had hurt me. Why should I make them feel good? Why should I let them off the hook? I understand now that forgiving someone else and letting go — when I am truly ready — dissolves the resentment that is stored within me. I will not jump to forgiveness too quickly, forcing myself to do what I am not sincerely able to do. I will not forgive because it is the right thing to do. I will fully feel and acknowledge all that blocks me, and I will give myself the time I need to do this. When I do forgive, it will be to set myself free, to let go of the past and to put it behind me.

I forgive to free myself.

Not seven but seventy times seven.

Matthew 18:22

Personal Growth

Today I see excitement and beauty in my own personal journey inward. Personal growth makes my life worth living. There is nothing like the feeling of expanding within. Self-knowledge is truly the road to a kind of realization of what life is really all about. I am my own personal road map. By solving the seemingly complex problems that life has presented me, I come closer to my self and my Higher Power. My sense of purpose in my life comes from an inner recognition and alignment with the beauty of life and an acceptance that life is meant to be lived and enjoyed.

My life is for me to enjoy.

I know nothing — I have
read nothing — and I mean to follow
Solomon's directions, "Get learning —
get understanding."

John Keats

Today I will practice the concept of non-attachment in my affairs. I recognize that my idea of ownership is an illusion. The things of this world are here for me to use and when I am finished, to pass them on to someone else to care for. When I am overly attached to people, places and things and something goes wrong with any of them, I assume I have gone wrong. It is one of life's paradoxes that I can love better if I am less identified with the object of my love. I am something eternal that can never be destroyed. I am a part of a higher energy that unites all things.

*I am identified not with what I see
but with who I am spiritually.*

Make up your mind . . . before it is too late, that the fitting thing for you to do is to live as a mature man who is making progress, and let everything which seems to be best for you be a law that must not be transgressed . . .

Epictetus

Honesty

Today I see that I can't release something just because someone tells me that it is the right or nice thing to do. Until I have moved through an internal process of identifying and communicating honestly what is going on with me, I can't really let it go. Honesty means that I am willing to be responsible. Whatever negative characteristics may have become a part of me from living in a dysfunctional home are, unfortunately, mine to deal with now. Projecting and blaming will not get me closer to getting rid of them. If I do not own my feelings — they will own me.

*Within my own mind and heart,
I am honest.*

I desire you would use all your skill to paint my picture truly like me; but remark all these roughnesses, pimples, warts and everything as you see me, otherwise I will not pay a farthing for it.

Oliver Cromwell to Peter Lely

Letting go of the past and moving on is a tall order; it requires a kind of releasing that I still find difficult to do. My past will always be in the shadows of my memory to haunt me if I do not recognize it as a part of me. If I pretend it's not important, grit my teeth and force myself to numb the pain, I have missed the point of recovery. On the other hand, if I am unwilling to let go no matter how many times I have worked through certain issues, I am also not allowing myself to be fully healthy and return to life. Part of recovery is a flowing through the stored pain and part is a decisive, forward-moving action.

I see the full picture of recovery and my responsibility to let go and move on.

———

Our concern is not how to worship in the catacombs but how to remain human in the skyscrapers.

Abraham Joshua Heschel

Releasing Relationships

Today I accept that I may not be able to take all of my relationships into recovery with me. As deeply as I desire to stay connected to certain people, I see now that it may not be possible. There are strong bonds that I forged during times of great pain while in my own disease. If I really recover and let go of the huge inner storehouse of anger and resentment, I may lose some of what held me in these relationships. Sometimes relationships will grow with me, sometimes they will not. Each person needs to be growing for change to happen. It is all right for me to recognize this and move on — it can even be the kind thing to do. I need not move on by rupturing the entire relationship; sometimes space or detachment is all that is needed.

*I am willing to change painful,
nonproductive relationships.*

———

Better a tooth out than always aching.
                                                Thomas Fuller

Today I recognize that I tend to produce in my life what I feel is true for myself. Thoughts have a creative power of their own, and if I look closely I can see my thoughts come to life. I create the possibility of what I would like by first experiencing it in my mind. I will visualize what I would like to have in my life in my mind's eye. I will accept what I see in my inner eye as being there for me and I will fully participate in my vision as if it were mine. I will be specific about what I see, smell, taste and feel, and accept it as fully as possible. I will enjoy my vision, then let it go and move on in my day, releasing it with no thought of controlling it further. I will let it happen if it is right for me in God's time.

All good things are possible for me.

———

If one advances confidently in the direction of his dreams, and endeavors to live the life which he has imagined, he will meet with a success unexpected in common hours.

Henry David Thoreau

The Witness

Today I will become aware of that part of me that is separate and observes all that I say, do, think and feel. I have a witness within me that can become a very useful part of my life. To be able to watch my behavior with a little bit of objectivity will help me to see myself as I really am. I will look with a compassionate eye. Just as I know it is not right to hurt others intentionally, it is equally not right to hurt myself. I recognize the godlike nature within me and others — we are all a part of the same Higher Power. By allowing my mind to watch itself with no thought of controlling or participating, I can learn a great deal about the way I work.

*I am an uncritical observer
of my own self.*

---

*Nothing in life is to be feared.
It is only to be understood.*

Marie Curie

Today I will allow my mind to connect with the mind of a Higher Power. The best things in life are free. I have the same access to a universal mind that anyone does. I will create quiet time in my day. I see that my mind can live where it chooses to live, that hanging on is not the answer, that letting go is. My mind can travel — it is not bound to the confines of my body. Just as water seeks its own level if it is undisturbed, so my mind will become quiet if I stop agitating it or allowing every little thing to throw me. I am the keeper of my own peace and today I recognize the influence I have over myself.

I can create inner change.

Those who make peaceful revolution impossible will make violent revolution inevitable.

John F. Kennedy

Negative Thoughts

Today I recognize that anything I grant myself, I grant to others, and that anything I grant to others, I grant to myself. What I believe of someone else, I believe of myself. Any harm I consider doing to anyone, I first have to conceive in my own mind where that thought will live and breathe and take root. I am connected to all people on an invisible plane. When we believe that we are only bodies, we believe that we are separate. But we are also mind and spirit and in this way flow in and out of one another's space. Today I know that what I create in my own mind about me or anyone else is what I live with. I first need to decide if carrying negative thoughts will be worth the disturbance and loss of serenity that they will cause me.

I take a good look at what
negativity costs me.

Hating people is like burning down your
own house to get rid of a rat.

Harry Emerson Fosdick

Today I realize that my perfectionism is born out of anxiety and a desire to maintain a sense of control. In a dysfunctional household one feels lost and out of control — there is a subtle sense of chaos in the atmosphere that feels as if it can erupt at any time. One tries to do things perfectly to keep trouble at bay. I am in charge of my own life today. My perfectionism gets in the way of spontaneity and my control does not let me live a day at a time. Recovery is not only about working through old feelings. It is also about recognizing dysfunctional patterns and letting them go. The dysfunctional patterns are control and perfectionism. I am willing to experience difficult feelings without swinging into action with my defensive behaviors.

I am able to feel feelings as they happen and to be spontaneous.

———

The artist who aims at perfection in everything achieves it in nothing.

Eugene Delacroix

Grief

*T*oday I will allow myself to enter into the dark and searing pain of my past and cry it all out. Much of the compulsion and perfectionism I live out in my life today is an attempt to bind my deep grief and keep it from surfacing. If my unconscious carries a silent wound, I will always be black and blue inside. I will not be able to approach situations with open eyes for fear they will trigger that unfelt pain. The grief that I carry hidden in silence has great power over my life and my relationships. I am willing today to experience those feelings in the present and release them. There is no longer any safety for me in hiding. My security comes from full awareness and acceptance of who I am. Until I understand my grief and allow myself to know it, I will not be free of its grip.

I am strong enough to grieve.

---

*Let mourning stop when one's grief
is fully expressed.*

Confucius

Decisions can be made and changed. I can make decisions today without feeling that my entire well-being is held in the balance each time. The anxiety that arises in me when I contemplate change is not more than I can tolerate. The risk involved in decision making need not feel unmanageable. Sometimes the idea of making any decision, big or small, is so overwhelming to me that I don't make one at all. I just let circumstances impose their will on me. I recognize now that I can participate in steering my own course if I am willing. I no longer need to know the outcome before I am capable of making a decision — no one knows that. The outcome of any decision rests on a number of variables. The decision rests on me.

I can make decisions that affect my life.

———

We lose the fear of making decisions, great and small, as we realize that should our choice prove wrong, we can, if we will, learn from the experience.

Bill W.

My Own Response

Today I recognize that there is little to be gained by letting other people's actions dictate my reactions. If I feel I have to respond in kind, I know that I will be hurting myself and wasting my time. When I feel someone is attacking me, I would do well to consider the source before I react. If I am willing to forego revenge, I may be able to see a cowardly or provocative act toward me for what it really is. Do I really need to convince the other person of what I see? Or might it not be enough just to escape the situation with my own peace of mind in tact?

I am in charge of my own response.

———

Don't let them push your buttons. The one trying to get you angry wants to control you. If you meet a negative approach positively, you are not letting the climate get out of your hands. . . .

Gerard I. Nierenberg

Today I see that my life is up to me. How I choose to live, what I will accomplish, how I conduct my intimate relationships and how I treat myself are in my own hands. I am no longer afraid that pain and anxiety will return me to a state of helplessness and vulnerability. Let it come — I am ready to meet it head-on. I am strong in the awareness that I can live as I choose to live. I have been willing to walk a path of recovery that, though difficult, has built a strength in me and a knowledge that I can survive my most painful feelings. I do not need to be afraid of my life if I am not afraid of myself or an emotional death. I have met and tamed the monsters that live inside of me. I am comfortable in my own skin.

I am free to be who I am.

Do well and you will have no need for ancestors.

Voltaire

Possibility

Today I allow myself to believe in possibility. There is more out there than meets my eye. If I allow my mind to cast itself outward and imagine options and potentials, I will be putting the wheels of inner change into motion. In order for my life to improve I need to be able to imagine alternatives to current behavior and in order to do that I need to trust in something that I cannot see. When I go fishing, I cast my line far out. I know that fish are out there somewhere. Today I will do the same with my mind — I will cast it out and trust that something is there. Even though I can't see the fish in the water, they are there. Even though I can't see possibility, it is there.

I trust in possibility.

---

*You have to believe in happiness or
happiness never comes.*

Douglas Malloch

Letting In Good

Today I am willing to allow my life to be good. Now that I have faced my pain, denial, delusion and resentment I have cleared out the debris and deadwood that kept me in an arm's-length relationship with life. Today I see clearly that I was a person filled with anger and hurt and that those feelings kept me from being able to live a normal life. Now I find I am afraid to let my life feel too good. I am, through my recovery, in a position to have a reasonably happy life, but the thought of allowing myself to count on that fills me with anxiety. I have felt so deeply let down in my past that allowing myself to trust again feels like walking through a brick wall or falling down a dark well. I will hold my own hand today and move through my own darkness toward the light, knowing that life holds no guarantees at any time.

I can live without guarantees.

I look to the hills from whence doth my help come. My help cometh from the Lord.

Psalm 121:1–2

Faith

Today I cast my faith into the air, into space, toward the heavens and I believe good things are in store for me. I have tapes inside of me that are old, old, old. Now when I hear them playing, I hear them for what they are, and I release myself from the power they have had over my life. When I feel myself acting in the same old ways — playing out my scripted part — I will observe myself. Even if the situation feels worn out, I can be new inside. Even if I play my old role, I can look for little ways to change it. I do not need to lose myself in a role today. I can play it and not be it — the role no longer owns my soul.

I am able to make small changes.

If you believe, then you hang on. If you believe, it means you've got imagination, you don't need stuff thrown out for you in a blue-print, you don't have to face facts . . . What can stop you? If you don't make it today, it'll come in tomorrow.

Ruth Gordon

I am willing to grow up today. I want to become a mature person. Part of my disease caused me to remain immature. My unmet needs from childhood sat inside of me like hungry monsters feeding on anything I threw into them. In recovery I have learned to identify my needs and to meet them in healthier ways. I can prioritize and see my life with some perspective. I recognize that part of maturation is identifying the hungry child within and working intelligently and compassionately with her before she works her wrath on me. I can survive feeling needy today — this is part of my new maturity.

I can survive my painful feelings and remain intact.

———

One must liberate oneself . . . from complexities, from taking one's fate too much to heart, before being able to rejoice simply because one is alive and among the living.

Czeslaw Milosz

Tears

Today I recognize that tears are one of my tools for self-healing. Tears shed in grief actually have a different chemical makeup from tears shed in joy. I take this to mean that my body is releasing chemicals that it wants to release when I shed tears, which is another reason why I feel so much better after a good cry. Throughout my recovery there have been times when I have wept for what appeared to be no reason. Today when I have a fuller picture of my life, I recall all of the grief that I held in. I felt that if I began to cry, I would never stop — so I didn't cry at all. I allow myself the cleansing act of crying now, recognizing its inherent curative power, and I am able to tolerate another person's tears, knowing that they create a beautiful connection between the deeper self and the outer self.

I let myself have tears.

I would never trust a man who didn't cry;
he wouldn't be human.

Norman Schwarzkopf

Today I take responsibility for my thoughts about my life. If I am talking the talk of recovery but still beating myself up on the inside, believing that doom and gloom lie around the corner, then that is what will manifest in my life. The universe hears my thoughts loud and clear. If I believe in good things for myself and bad things for others, I am also in my own way of experiencing a better life. Believing in abundance for myself and scarcity for others will not work. If this is an abundant universe, it is an abundant universe for all. This is my truth today. Others' lives are as important as mine. I understand that what I believe to be true for me tends to show up in my life, so today I observe closely what I put out in thought form.

I watch my thoughts and observe their content.

What I believe about myself and about
my life becomes true for me.

Louise Hay

Befriending Feelings

Today I befriend my feelings without judgment. If I am still lonely or depressed, I need not act on that feeling, seeing it as unrecovered, then going through complicated mental machinations to change it. Instead I give it space and observe it, knowing that this process will have a transforming effect. I allow myself to feel other than what I am supposed to feel. I give room to a feeling and befriend it rather than push it away with impatient, intolerant thoughts. My feelings follow a pattern. Rather than control them, I simply watch as a feeling arises, intensifies, hangs around inside of me and lifts all of its own accord. I need not rush my own process of life today. I can be with it. I can allow it to be with me. I can be fully human and alive.

I observe my feeling process rather than control it.

Find the seed at the bottom of your heart and bring forth a flower.

Shigenori Kameoka

Today I create a new belief system for myself. In the process of recovery I have got in touch with, felt and released old pain and resentment, and I am in a healthier place now. Even though I am emotionally cleaner, I may still be hanging on to old beliefs that no longer serve me in my new life. Whenever I hear myself believing the worst, I will watch myself in action. I will observe that negative voice and allow myself fully to hear it and feel its effect on my psyche. I will notice with a compassionate eye where it seems to come from, then I will gently release it from my mind. I will allow a new, more affirmative message to emerge in that space and quietly repeat it until I feel its presence within me.

I can create new beliefs.

———

Make voyages! Attempt them . . . there's nothing else.

Tennessee Williams

Will

Today I rest quietly in the awareness that I am part of a compassionate universe. I turn my will over to the care of a loving God. In the past the idea of turning my will over seemed absolutely nuts until I came to believe that a power greater than myself could restore me to sanity. It's not so much a matter of giving up my will but aligning it with a higher one. It is a gesture of good faith, an act of trust. Today I understand the difference between willfulness and will. I let go of the willfulness, recognizing it to be encapsulating and often self-defeating, and I turn over my will, understanding that I cannot always see the whole picture and that I need to leave room for the unknown to work.

I trust and act accordingly.

Made a decision to turn our will and our lives over to the care of God as we understood Him.

Step 3, Alcoholics Anonymous

Changing Old Beliefs

Today I make room to change any beliefs that I may have about being unworthy or undeserving of good in my life. I accept the abundance of this universe, and I truly feel that I am part of it. I believe that life wants to give to me if I can let it. So often by insisting on the truth of my own negative thoughts I am my own worst enemy. I limit my growth with ideas and rules about how I won't be able to grow. Rather than take a chance at trying a new way of being and seeing, I stay with my old and familiar pattern, even if I hate it. Today I am willing to see the old for what it is and release it. I will allow something new to come in its place and see how I do with it.

I am capable of changing.

———

Let everyone try and find that as a result of daily prayer he adds something new to his life, something with which nothing can be compared.

Mohandas K. Gandhi

Affirmation

Today I see the difference between positive affirmations and negative affirmations. The voices inside my head that tell me I can't do something affirm that feeling over and over again until I come to believe it, and it becomes part of my personal belief system. I can choose to affirm myself in positive, loving ways. When I feel myself slip into old dysfunctional patterns of thinking, I will gently bring myself around to a more positive point of view. The positive things that I say to myself will seep down into my unconscious and plant seeds that will grow and multiply. I am ready to have the life that I envision for myself. I can live with being happy.

I affirm myself in positive ways.

Though thou hast ever so many counsellors, yet do not forsake the counsel of your own soul.

John Ray

I Got What I Got

Today I accept that I got what I got while growing up. Some was beneficial, some detrimental and some good enough. Whatever it was, it's what was and nothing can change that. Because I have been willing to confront the dysfunctional parts of myself and work through emotional blockages, I have also been able to reclaim my joy and strength. This process of recovery makes me stronger, more supple and tolerant, more appreciative of life. While once I had a thousand theories and no experience, now I have a thousand days of experience and no theories. Life simply is life. Trying to fit it into models and patterns only reduces it for me. I know that it is not that simple. All the same, I also know that it is nothing but simple. I can live at the center of the paradox.

I accept and experience life.

Bloom where you are planted.
Nancy Reader Companion's
Aunt Grace

Growing Gradually

Today I can go step by step and let in only what I can handle. My life does not have to look good and feel good every minute of the day. I can take breaks. It's okay to have a few semi-nourishing "zone-out" activities. Watching "Bonanza" or wandering mindlessly around the house is fine. Recovery is not about perfection; it's about feeling okay with myself so that I am in a better position to enjoy myself when I feel like it. I will not hound myself with unrealistic perfection. Normal is a little bit of everything.

I let myself be an everyday person.

———

Be willing to shed parts of your previous life. For example, in our 20s we wear a mask; we pretend to know more than we do. We must be willing as we get older to shed our cocktail party phoniness and admit, "I am who I am."

Gail Sheehy

Today I will not blackmail myself or others with my own neediness and I will not let others blackmail me with theirs. In recovery I have learned to identify my needs. Now in recovery I will learn that because I have identified them does not necessarily mean that they will all be met. Part of growing up is learning to tolerate my own neediness. Being demanding about what I want will not necessarily work for me to obtain it. This does not mean that I return to my old way of postponing my needs for so long that I actually lose track of what they are. It only means that I learn to take a mature and kind attitude toward them. Neither over-reacting nor under-reacting, I will give myself time to sit with my own being for a while to see what's really going on there.

I can deal with my needs in healthy ways.

―――――

The art of life lies in a constant readjustment to our surroundings.

Kakuzo Okakura

Freedom

Today I see that I need not cut myself off from my roots in order to be free. Rather, with full honesty and compassion, I need to recognize where I come from. My task in recovery is to return *myself* to health — not to fix or judge anyone else. When I am truly clean and clear inside — when I have been willing to look at and live with my full truth — there will be nothing to run away from. It is the fear and darkness in my own soul, that lives inside of me now and terrifies me the most. Who gave it to me no longer matters, it is mine now. It is this inner darkness that I need to dispel and shed light on. I will always come from somewhere and that is okay.

I accept things as they are.

Emancipation from the bondage of the soil is no freedom for the tree.
Rabindranath Tagore

I can change my thoughts. The thoughts that I think today are under my control. The thoughts that I think today are what I will see manifest in my life tomorrow. If I am changing thought patterns, it will take a degree of recognition and discipline on my part. The recognition lies in noticing how what I think manifests in my day to day life. How is what I expect in my life related to what actually happens? Today I acknowledge the creative power of my thoughts. Like a sculptor with raw clay who co-creates a work of art with the medium, I am the co-creator of my thoughts. I am the energy, and thought is my medium.

*I understand the role I play
in co-creating my reality.*

———

Nothing great is created suddenly, any more than a bunch of grapes or a fig. I answer you that there must be time. Let it first blossom, then bear fruit, then ripen.

Epictetus

Choosing A Road

Today I feel that I stand and look down at two roads. One road is the continuum of my past, the road that stems from all my yesterdays. The other is the road that I choose. It is less clear, wide open, a road on which I feel I have not traveled before, on which I am an explorer. Each day, many times, these two roads lay before me. One is obvious, one is new and unknown. I will choose the new road today. I will do what feels more challenging and exciting — less normal and comfortable. Comfort often brings me what I already have — good or bad. I will measure that kind of comfort today. I will give myself enough of it to feel stable and secure, but I will not suffocate myself in it. Life can have a wonderful feeling of adventure and today I will climb on board.

I choose my own road.

Do everything. One thing may turn out right.
                                          Humphrey Bogart

Healing Hurt Relationships

Today I will open myself to healing in my relationships. So much of life depends on the quality of intimacy with myself and so much of the quality of my intimacy is the quality of my relationships. It is synergistic. As my relationship with myself and my Higher Power gets better, my other relationships grow. Deep healing with people I care about has much more significance than might appear; it is soul- and life-transforming. I experience moments of quiet expansion when my heart and mind actually feel as if they are widening in all directions. Even though I cannot necessarily sustain this burst, part of it remains with me, integrates into my personality and becomes mine. I am willing to grow a step at a time and heal little by little.

I can heal hurt relationships.

Life is not living, but living in health.

Martial

Natural Growth

Today I recognize that my bursts of growth are accompanied by backslides and I accept this as a natural learning pattern. When children have a learning explosion into talking, walking or whatever, they experience a minor regression. When I have a learning or growth explosion, I may experience a regression afterward. New behaviors and awareness stabilize with practice. Today I will not take that regression to mean that the growth was not genuine. I will understand that accompanying a large step forward is a small step backward. I will allow this to take place, trusting that my experience of growth will integrate naturally if I allow it to.

I trust my natural pattern of growth and expansion.

Just don't give up trying to do what you really want to do. Where there's love and inspiration, I don't think you can go wrong.
Ella Fitzgerald

Today I understand that the purpose of forgiving is to release my own mind from the pain of held resentment. I do not forgive someone today because it is what nice people do. I forgive because it sets my mind free for other things — like living happily in the present. This is not to say that I do not acknowledge a painful relationship and past abuse. I have a right and a responsibility to set healthy boundaries for myself. Forgiving doesn't mean being close to someone I need to keep my distance from or trying to return to the past to rework it. Forgiving simply means that I am willing to live my life from today forward without unwittingly recreating and replaying old scripts that I hold in my unconscious. I forgive myself and others with understanding. It is my quickest road to freedom.

I am willing to be free.

———

Freedom lies in bold action.

Robert Frost

Letting Go Of Hurt

I let go of hurt today. When someone is hurting me, chances are I am also hurting them. To walk away conscious only of my own hurt binds me in mine. When I can't see the other side, I am jailed within my own, going over and over and over the same material. Real maturity sees both sides. It is not coldhearted. There are always two stories and today I choose not to get lost in my own from where I cannot see anything else. Resolution comes so much more easily when I am willing to be fair. Also, when I take responsibility for my own stuff, I leave what isn't mine within the other person. When I won't see mine, I cannot clearly see theirs, so I carry the weight of both.

I can separate issues today.

———

Don't look over other people's shoulders. Look in their eyes. Don't talk at your children. Take their faces in your hands and talk to them. Don't make love to a body, make love to a person.

Leo Buscaglia

Today I can reach out for help. When my mind turns in on itself and goes around and around tossing the same old thoughts up and watching them land, I will remind myself that I can reach out. Sometimes just the thought of reaching out is enough. It sets something into motion that opens a door or a window. I can also reach inside of myself to a Higher Power. That act creates an inner change. To envision reaching out in my mind makes room for change, for a shift, for something else. I do not need to think of reaching out today as a big act; just a little, sincere thought makes a difference. A willingness to see something in another way can open a path from within me.

I can reach out.

———

God dwells wherever men let Him in.

Martin Buber

Accepting Death

Today I accept my own mortality and the mortality of others. While I fight the reality of death, I also misunderstand the reality of life. Life, whether we accept it or not, is temporary. When we do not know this inside, we live as if we had all the time in the world. While this is not necessarily bad, it has the tendency to dull our senses and make us unappreciative of all the richness and potential that lie around us now. When we are willing to know that death is looking over our shoulder, life becomes sweeter. It becomes not so much a question of wasting time as of appreciating time and recognizing what time is.

I make peace with my temporary visit on earth.

It was the Psalmist, one of the world's wisest men, who prayed, "So teach us to number our days, that we may apply our hearts unto wisdom." The fact is, we cannot truly face life until we have learned to face the fact that it will be taken away from us.

Billy Graham

Risking Change

Today I recognize that all growth requires change, that all change includes risk and that these are scary and difficult. If I am not experiencing discomfort in my feelings, then I am not really changing. Deep meaningful change is hard won; it is not easy. It requires courage and commitment. When I am not willing to take any risks, when I only choose to stay safe, my life becomes progressively more narrow. When I am not willing to risk being hurt, my relationships become more shallow. When I am not willing to search for a Higher Power, I have to make-do with the stories and descriptions of other people's God.

***I have the courage and willingness
to change.***

Observe always that everything is the result of change, and get used to thinking that there is nothing Nature loves so well as to change existing forms and make new ones like them.

Marcus Aurelius

Meditation

Today I set aside time for my spiritual growth through increasing my *conscious* contact with my Higher Power. I create enough quiet space in my day so that I can hear more than the noise around me. I get quiet enough so that the voice of God within me can speak. I allow myself to know what I know and see what I see. Spirituality does not, as I may have been taught, drop out of the sky. It grows and deepens through conscious effort on my part. I can write, read good books, meditate or dwell on higher thoughts as a way to encounter and be with my greater self within. Whatever works to increase my feeling of spiritual presence is right.

I pay attention to my spiritual life.

———

Sought through prayer and meditation to improve our conscious contact with God.

Step 11, Alcoholics Anonymous

*T*oday I recognize that I must have a self before I can lose a self. In the process of development, children harden their boundaries first before they make choices about where to soften them. In recovery the same process takes place. I reach back and rework areas in my life when I was not allowed to develop my own boundaries. This may be either because they were constantly invaded in little ways or because my family had hard boundaries around it to protect its secrecy. Within those boundaries, identities tend to be fused. We had a family identity but lacked individual ones, an innocent mistake given the times. I am patient with myself today as I develop a self and learn about what I am like.

I have my own personality.

———

There is nothing noble
about being superior to some other person.
The true nobility is in being superior
to your previous self.

Hindustani proverb

Blame

March 2

Today I see that blame doesn't work. It doesn't work for two reasons. One, no one really escapes from a family illness and gets better until they identify the illness that is within them. This is particularly true as I get older. It doesn't matter anymore where the illness came from; what matters is how it works inside of me and what I do from there. Two, blaming someone else only keeps the focus off of me. The way for me to get and stay well is to keep the focus on myself, to learn who I am and to develop my own self. When I blame, I postpone my own recovery, and all the recovery that I have attained cannot serve me when my attention and mind are on someone else.

I recognize that blame doesn't work.

Never look down on anybody unless you're helping him up.

Jesse Jackson

Today I understand that family illness is a co-creation. A family disease is a dynamic. Each time one person gets sicker, the dynamic can get sicker, and each time one person gets healthier, the dynamic can get healthier because each person's input is important. In a sick family the "elephant in the living room" is a sick elephant. The disease becomes a large container in the center of the family in which painful feelings, such as shame, anger, resentment and fear, live, breathe and grow. Each person lives with the presence of this container, and each person is affected by it. Those who think that this container affects only a few family members are kidding themselves.

I accept my family illness and my part in it.

———

Whatever games are played with us, we must play no games with ourselves, but deal in our privacy with the last honesty and truth.

Ralph Waldo Emerson

Healing

Today I have faith in healing. I have experienced more healing both in myself and in my relationships than I ever thought possible. Recovery is a process. I have known in my past serious dysfunction that derailed my relationships. The lack of commitment, the hurt, the alienation and the resentment I experienced seemed too much to ever overcome. But I have witnessed many small miracles. Conversations and connections that I never thought would happen. Love that I never thought I would feel or be given. I have wanted this healing deep in my heart, and today I understand that wanting it and envisioning it were enough to set the wheels in motion. Willingness was what allowed me to be there and accept it when the time was right.

*I am capable of healing in
my relationships.*

---

*Above all, do not lose your
desire to walk.*

Sören Kierkegaard

Today when I encounter my own resistance, I will not turn back or be hard on myself. Instead I will see it as a sign that I am beginning to change. If I did not encounter my own resistance, I would not really be working or taking seriously what I am doing. Resistance is a sign that something is happening. When I am asking myself to change the way I see things and adopt a more positive, constructive attitude, a lot of old tapes kick in and tell me that it can't be done, it won't be worth it, it will all fall apart anyway, I will just fail, make things worse, be kidding myself, etc. I can recognize these old tapes for what they are, and my resistance to growth and change becomes a sign that growth and change are beginning to take place.

I accept my own fear of change.

———

*Resistance is the first
step to change.*

Louise Hay

Life Is An Adventure

Today I remind myself that life is an adventure. There are no guarantees that anything will turn out as expected. My best-laid plans are turned upside down in an instant if life so chooses. Life is constant change. The things that I expected to go one way go another. Even if the outside of my life appears stable, there is a constant subtle movement — times that are very different, tasks and jobs that change with the years, passages that I go through as I age. If I regard life as an adventure, perhaps I will try less hard to clench it in my fist and I will hold it with a more open hand. My co-dependency tells me that every time something in my life changes I am also going to be somehow different. I identify with a stable place within, and not in the things around me.

**_I can adjust to change without
losing myself._**

———

*Life is what happens to you when
you're making other plans.*

John Lennon

Today I accept that love is not a sentiment but an energy. When I see love in a sentimental context, I wait for the situation to appear before I allow myself to experience the feeling. The energy of love is always available to me. I can consciously allow it to pass through me and surround me. I can wrap myself in an experience of love and send it out to others. I can call on this energy in times of need and use it to heal myself physically, mentally and spiritually. When I think and feel love, I connect with those energies around me — I allow myself to be with a loving universe. What I feel inside is my business. Why not give love a try in the privacy of my own mind and heart?

I attract an energy of love.

Love heals. . . . Love is the most powerful known stimulant to the immune system.

Bernie S. Siegel

Willingness

Today I am willing for healing to take place in ruptured relationships. I have been doing the best that I can. My acknowledgment that I may have hurt someone else in no way disparages me. I have also been hurt, and I extend the same understanding to myself that I do to others. We have all been doing the best that we can. My willingness to make amends speaks to my spiritual growth and desire for honesty. Making amends to others sets things straight with myself. My self-respect is growing to the extent that I am no longer comfortable with unfinished business. I will finish up my side for my own self and allow the rest to be where it is. It is for myself that I make amends; I do not need to control the result.

I am willing to feel clean inside.

———

Made a list of all persons we had harmed and became willing to make amends to them all.
Step 8, Alcoholics Anonymous

Today I understand that to study myself in earnest is to study life, people and the universe. To see it as anything less is to lose myself in the tangle of my own head and thoughts. I have wondered if studying myself was self-centered and narcissistic. I realize that it is only when I don't see that I am connected to all of life and to the universe that I am in danger of becoming overly self-involved because I miss the crucial point. The same road map toward truth that is in me is in all people and by studying myself I study humanity. My window on the world is within my own soul.

I sincerely study myself.

The questions that one asks oneself begin, at last, to illuminate the world and become one's key to the experience of others.

James Baldwin

Having A Self

Today I live with the understanding that
no matter what happens in my life — who
stays, who leaves, what my circumstances
are — there is one person who will not leave
me and that is me. I have a self today. I lost
myself to disease, to living, to the thousands
of daily decisions and activities that became
my life and my sense of self. When I needed
to come home to me, I was not there. I didn't
know what I thought or felt. I couldn't tell
what was going on inside of me. I didn't
know when I called out my name who would
answer. I have worked hard to find me
again. I can separate my disease from who I
really am. Today I know that I am the one
person I can count on and trust to stay with
me. I know that as long as I have my self, I
can handle the rest.

I have a self.

———

To thine own self be true
And it shall follow as the night follows the day
Thou canst not be false to any other man.
William Shakespeare

70

Higher Power Within Me

Today I recognize that a Higher Power lives and breathes inside of me, through me, as me. I used to think that God was the chairperson of somebody else's board, and I spent my time in search of another person's version of a Higher Power. But really there is no searching — it feels more like an acceptance. That is the well-kept secret that God lives, not in the heavens or inside special buildings but within my very self. My direct access to myself is my direct access to my Higher Power and my estrangement from myself is my estrangement from my Higher Power. We are co-creators, hand in glove, a team. Today I see it as an act of surrender, acceptance and love.

I love my Higher Power and my Higher Power loves me — we are one.

You've always had the power [to return home] right there in your shoes, you just had to learn it for yourself.
Frank L. Baum, *The Wizard of Oz*

Giving Up Fixing My Family

March 12

Today I give up trying to fix my family of origin so that I can get on with having a happy life. I have seen it as my duty, my cause, my need, etc., when perhaps it has really been just one more place to hide my sickness. What would be the worst thing that could happen if I got well and happy? Just the thought terrifies me — I feel sure I wouldn't know how to act and I would embarrass myself in front of saner people than I. I feel I could not sustain it, that I would be carrying too much shame inside of me and I would always feel somehow different than happier people. I feel I wouldn't be good enough to meet the occasion. So really, fixing my family has been a way of denying that I have these other feelings. Today I can feel my shame and sense of inadequacy and move through it.

I can only live my own life.

———

What you dislike in another
take care to correct in yourself.

Thomas Sprat

Letting Go Of Shame

Today I become willing to see, feel and release the shame that keeps me tied to dysfunction. There was always a bad guy in my family of origin. We searched in cooperative silence for one person on whom to pin the family disease. When that person was removed either by death or circumstance, we found another. We could not function without a fall guy. If we were unable to find one among ourselves, we talked about someone else. We didn't understand that making someone the bad guy made us all the bad guy. Our fear of being identified as the sick one was so great we had to pin it on someone else. Today I look at myself.

*I can live through feelings of
shame and let them go.*

———

*Confront the dark parts of yourself and
work to banish them with illumination and
forgiveness. Your willingness to wrestle with
your demons will cause your angels to sing.*
Angus Wilson

Self-Love

Today I love myself. So much of what our culture says tells me that loving myself is somehow wrong and that love of things acquired and outside of myself is what I should want. What I have learned, though, is that no matter how much I have, if I have no self I am wholly unable to experience or enjoy anything. Loving myself is part of having myself because that which I do not love tends to disappear and leave my life. Even my self, if unloved long enough, will go away. That which I love tends to grow and become more present. My self is all I really have, everything else comes and goes. I will take care of what I have.

It is all right to love myself.

———

To love oneself is the beginning of a lifelong romance.

Oscar Wilde

Trusting My Inner Voice

Today I will trust my own heart. The clear message that whispers within me has more to tell me than a thousand voices. I have a guide within me who knows what is best for me. There is a part of me that sees the whole picture and knows how it all fits together. My inner voice may come in the form of a strong sense, a pull from within, a gut feeling or a quiet knowing. However my inner voice comes to me, I will learn to pay attention. In my heart I know what is going on. Though I am conditioned from childhood to listen to others, today I recognize that it is deeply important for me to hear what I am saying from within.

I will trust my inner voice.

———

There is no purifier like knowledge in this world: Time makes man find himself in his heart.

Bhagavadgita

Responsibility

Today I clearly see that the secret of mental health lies in taking responsibility for my own stuff and minding my own business. As long as I am making other people's affairs my affairs, I am removing myself from my own point of power which lies within me. The control that I think I have over others is an illusion, a mirage. The only person I have control over is myself, and trying to manipulate the lives and minds of others sabotages my own serenity. There is no one in this world better equipped to understand me than me. I know myself more intimately than anyone else will ever know me. If I am willing to own my own stuff, my part of the problem, my strong and weak points, not only will I release myself from my mental fog, but I will have the gift of seeing clearly what part of the problem does not belong to me.

I am responsible for me.

Keep the focus on yourself.

12-Step slogan

Today when I look at a sunset and wish I were with someone else or feel that I cannot fully enjoy a beautiful view all by myself, I will remember that I am never alone. I will allow the emptiness inside of me to be filled with my Higher Power, however I conceive that to be. Together we will enjoy the sunset and the soft splashing of the waves against the rocks. I am my own point of power, all of my life passes through me and in this sense I am always alone. At the same time God is coded into all of my being; there is no difference between me and this universal energy or force. In this sense I am never alone — I am always connected. Like a cool summer rain or the soft glow of sunset, my Higher Power dwells within me.

I am never alone.

The force cannot be seen. It is all around us, it goes through us, inside us outside . . . it is always with you.

George Lucas, *Star Wars*

Affirmations

Today I will think of one thing about myself that I would like to change or see growth in, and I will make my own affirmation. It may be, "I am grateful for my beautiful and healthy body," "I manage my affairs with confidence and competence" or anything else that fits for me. All that I need to do is repeat it to myself and accept it as true for me. I let my unconscious do the rest. The unconscious is a marvelous thing. It is always busy recreating what it believes to be true. I have witnessed often enough how my unconscious continually reproduces my deepest fears and anxieties in my life. Today I use this power consciously and for my betterment.

*I send positive
messages to my unconscious and
trust the process.*

———

Sink in thyself! There ask what ails thee at that shrine!

Matthew Arnold

78

Today I understand the true meaning of amends. An amends is not to make the other person feel good or to make a ruptured relationship suddenly fine. It is not an effective way of getting what I want. An amends is an attempt to free my own mind and heart of a burden that I no longer wish to carry. It is a recognition of my commitment to my own emotional sobriety. When I make an amends to someone with whom I need to clear out some unfinished business, I gracefully disengage myself from the tangled mass of reciprocal resentment. How my amends will be received is not up to me to control. The amends I make are for myself — another person's response is out of my jurisdiction.

An amends is made to free me.

Forgiveness is the answer to the child's dream of a miracle by which what is broken is made whole again, what is soiled is again made clean.

Dag Hammarskjold

Inner Belief

I believe in this world; it is the place that I have been born into, and I love the breeze and the grass, the sky and the water. I have an intimate exchange with nature — like a lover, I feel held and nourished by it. I believe in people; they are the species I belong to. I recognize that underneath our superficial differences we all want and need the same things. I believe that truth and goodness will prevail. I have experienced and seen more healing than I thought would ever happen. I feel good with little gains. I see small things as deeply meaningful and I am moved by a power that I cannot explain but that I sense inside and out. Today I feel good.

I believe in life.

———

Being unwanted, unloved, uncared for, forgotten by everybody; I think that is a much greater hunger, a much greater poverty than the person who has nothing to eat . . . we must find each other.

Mother Teresa

Co-dependency

Today I recall that being co-dependent in my thinking removes me from my own center. When I am living in charge of myself, I can manage. When I am constantly preoccupied with what others are thinking and feeling, my life begins to feel unmanageable for the simple reason that I cannot manage anyone but myself. There is no such thing as walking in someone else's shoes, and even if I knew how to manage things better than they, it would not be within my power to do so. Co-dependency is really a misguided attempt to do someone else's living for them or vice versa. The other side effect is that when I am busy attempting to operate the controls in someone else, no one is operating mine.

I can sit at my own controls.

One must learn to love oneself . . . with a wholesome and healthy love, so that one can bear to be with oneself and need not roam.

Friedrich Nietzsche

Come To Believe

Today I know that recovery happens in layers — like peeling an onion. Sometimes when I am working on a new layer, I feel as if I am back to square one, and I get down on myself for being in that place again. I need to remind myself that although the layers are different, the process is the same. Each time I work through new material, I move through all the stages of the growth process. With each new area of recovery and growth, I am powerless over the strength of the feelings that are mobilized within me. Each time I need to realize that this process will restore me to sanity; each time I need to turn it over. The 12-Step program and recovery have given me a place to go with my most painful feelings so that I can genuinely accept and work through them.

I accept recovery as a process.

———

We admitted we were powerless over alcohol [emotions, dysfunction] — that our lives had become unmanageable.

Step 1, Alcoholics Anonymous

Talking Things Over

Today I recognize that it is actually possible to talk things over. To be direct and honest with a person with the intention of working out a problem seems difficult and risky. I still feel that my honest feelings will be met with hostility and that somehow I will end up creating a mess. I experienced this as powerlessness when I was young and I felt unable to do anything to change my situation. Today I know a new kind of powerlessness. It comes from a mature understanding that I cannot control another person. I can only keep my side clean and honest. There is no need for me to be blamed nor do I need to blame the other person. If I enter the dialogue willing to be honest and open-minded, refraining from insults and criticism, chances are pretty good that something will get resolved.

I am able to talk things over.

Speech is a mirror of the soul: as a man speaks, so is he.

Publilius Syrus

Inside My Mind

Today I am grateful to feel alive and to recognize that life is a spiritual journey. All of my circumstances in life are spiritual challenges if I choose to look at them that way. Getting free of my own over-attachment to people, places, things and ideas, mistaking them for me, releases my spirit. Once my spirit is released, it can travel and experience the real beauty of life. Life surrounds me; it is inside, outside and everywhere. If I am free and still inside, life is there. If I am not ruminating and filling my mind with unnecessary preoccupations — life is there, spirit is there — waiting to be seen and felt.

I allow my mind its freedom.

---

*There is one spectacle grander
than the sea, that is the sky; there is
one spectacle grander than the sky,
that is the interior of the soul.*

Victor Hugo

There are no "buts" today. I am what I am, others are what they are, life is what it is. I will not parenthesize my growth with a "but" or hold back my forward-moving spirit with second guesses, for today I am living with things as they are. I am exactly where I am meant to be, learning what I need to learn. All I need do is move through situations with willingness to learn and openness to feel. When feelings are brought up, I can accept them as what is happening within me — no need to resist and analyze them. Transformation will happen in the moving through and the acceptance of them. I trust that my life is unfolding in such a way that what I need to learn will be before me.

I am willing to learn.

What one knows is, in youth,
of little moment; they know enough
who know how to learn.

Henry Adams

The Mystery

Today I accept that part of myself that will never be satisfied and I comfort and tame it. There is a place in me that knows it will never know. At times I can get depressed about that and feel that there's no real point to life. But I am beginning to feel that to accept and love this side of myself is what also gives life beauty and meaning. Perhaps meaning is not knowing and understanding, but an acceptance of the mystery, an embracing of the unknown. After all, it is that mystery that gives even the most ordinary circumstance an eternal sort of glow — a sense of depth, a feeling that there is more.

I accept that I will never fully understand
— I embrace the mystery.

———

The soul is restless and furious;
it wants to tear itself apart and cure
itself of being human.

Ugo Betti

Today I see that the bitterness I carry around for someone else is living and breathing inside my own mind. It is impossible for me to feel anything for someone else that I do not feel first within myself. In order to project a feeling onto anyone, I need to first create that feeling inside of me. Today I ask myself if the person I am hating is worth it. Is it worth putting aside my own peace of mind and potential for joy to feel this negative feeling? It is one thing to acknowledge honestly my difficult repressed feelings, but there is a difference between acknowledging and experiencing feelings for my own edification and creating them again and again for the sake of reprisal.

I need not create bitterness.

Heat not a furnace for your own foe so hot,
That it do singe yourself.

William Shakespeare

Changing Behavior

Today I take a position outside of the family illness. If I keep trading injury for injury, insult for insult, there will be no end to it. Sooner or later one of us has to stop and it might as well be me. This doesn't mean that I lay myself wide open and take abuse. It only means that I recognize the futility of this going back and forth over the same old ground again and again. It will not cure or heal anything. It only gives a temporary vent to hurt and resentment, but in doing so it keeps me bound to those feelings. Though I may not wish to make nice or try to fix, I can give up my end of the mudslinging, that in itself would be enough.

I can lay down the sword.

Blood cannot be washed out with blood.
Persian proverb

Today I will make an effort not to make someone else the cause of my discomfort. Why should I spend my time finding fault with others for things that are probably also problems in me? It really is not up to me to wander around the world judging everyone else. Not only does it make me someone who people want to avoid, but it also keeps me from seeing myself clearly. Judging gets no one anywhere. When I put out that kind of energy toward others, they are more likely to return it to me in kind, thus I create an atmosphere of criticism for myself to live in. Wouldn't it be nicer today if I left the judging for someone else and I just lived?

I see that judgment gets me nowhere.

They have a right to censure that have a heart to help.

William Penn

Giving

Today I recognize the difference between giving so that I will get it back and giving what I wish to receive. When I give with strings, I am already disappointing both the receiver and myself — the receiver because from the beginning it doesn't feel like a gift and me because I will never get back what I really want. When I give freely, I am taking a risk and trusting; I am entering into an act of good faith and people feel that. In my past I too often gave out of fear or to smooth things over. No matter what I gave from this place, it was not enough to do the job — I couldn't make things work. I will separate the past from the present today and know that my giving is within my control. I am not giving so that my safety will be assured; I am giving out of love.

I give because I choose to give.

———

To give and then not to feel that one has given is the very best of all ways of giving.

Max Beerbohm

Separating The Disease Out

Today I am able to separate the disease from the person. People change — I have changed. The same person who was a terror to me in childhood could possibly be a friend today. We were all sick, no one really escaped our family disease. The disease that kept us from one another in childhood need not keep me from having what I can have today, both with myself and others. I can see who I was as a person with a disease, and I can see who I am as a person without one. If I am going to have some of the people in my life today who have hurt me in the past and who I have hurt, I need to forgive each of us for not knowing better, for being sick.

I can separate the disease from the person.

———

"Wait," says an Arab proverb, "and stay at your window; you will see your enemy's corpse pass by." I am not a man to harbor grudges and I prefer to say: "Wait, open your door and you will see an old enemy come in who has become your dear friend."

André Maurois

Getting What I Want

*T*oday I see that getting what I want is a moment-to-moment affair. There is no list of ten things that I want and need to get, and even getting those ten things will not necessarily bring me any closer to happiness than I am now. What I want is something from inside myself. I built up walls in childhood to keep out the hurt and the bad — unfortunately today they keep out the good. They keep me from taking in what gives me a feeling of being whole, content, happy and safe. It is my task to gently remove these walls. The ounces and pounds will get through into that hungry place and will begin to fill it from within.

I can let in good.

The desire for imaginary benefits often involves the loss of present blessings.

Aesop

Leaving Perfectionism

Today I know that I need not like everything about someone to enjoy having them in my life. As a child I may have felt defective in some fundamental way. No matter what I did to improve myself and love those around me, the situation only got worse. This made my self-esteem drop and my drive toward perfectionism increase. I could not relax and let myself be who I was and others be who they were. I was worried that it would not be good enough. This has made me picky and judgmental, both with myself and with those close to me. I have trouble tolerating small infractions — I want things to be perfect. Today I recognize that perfection is an illusion, that learning to accept people as they are, myself as I am and life one day at a time brings the safety that I used to think control would bring.

I let go of my need for perfection.

Striving to better, oft we mar what's well.

William Shakespeare

Taking My Freedom

Today I allow myself to have the recovery and happiness I am capable of, whether or not my family of origin or current family has them. My need to fix everyone else before I can give myself permission to grow comes straight out of a dysfunctional past. I was afraid that if I separated from my family, I would lose them. Fixing them kept me feeling connected. Today I see this for what it is, and I can allow myself to take my own freedom without expecting understanding and recognition for what I am doing. I have many sources from which to get love and support. My family can give me what they can give me. I need not force out more.

Today I grow as much as I can envision.

———

The virtue of a free man appears
equally great in refusing to face difficulties
as in overcoming them.

Baruch Spinoza

Today I recognize my denial of the past for what it was. When I was very small, I felt powerless. I could not see traumatic events with any perspective. To me, the sky was falling and my very survival was threatened. In order to make these events tolerable I used my child's magical thinking. I wove a web of stories that made me feel better about what was happening in my home. I confused myself because, instead of feeling my painful feelings, I covered them over and made them the way I wished they were. My denial was my way of making my life livable, a misguided attempt at positive thinking. What I didn't know was that my denial would cost me my truth and that the truth would still live inside of me whether or not I saw it. Today I can see clearly and live with my life as it was and is.

Today I see my life clearly.

———

He who knows others is learned;
He who knows himself is wise.

Lao-tzu

Responsible Behavior

Today I keep my own house clean and let go of the rest — some of the ways that I wish to live as a recovered person will not be readily understood by others. I will keep my own scorecard clean and not worry about the results. I will act in a way that makes it easier for me to live with myself — that keeps my own conscience clear. Other people's negative projections of me no longer run me. I am the one who makes the decisions about who I want to be. I need not defend and explain myself again and again. I need not ask permission to be who I am. I allow myself to be happy in my own skin today and think well of myself, no matter what others think of me.

I create my own self.

A thief believes everyone steals.
Edgar Watson Howe

Today I will light one candle and that candle is myself. I will keep my own flame burning. I turn my sight to light and love and goodness. For today there is no need to be discouraged. So what if I see and identify all the ills of society and diagnose it as sick — what good will that do me or anyone else? I heal society by healing myself. Just as life is lived one day at a time, the world will heal one person at a time. Each time I think a positive, loving thought, it goes into the ether and vibrates. This is nothing particularly mystical; I have but to sit near someone and look at their face to feel how their thoughts affect me. I take ownership of my own inner workings and their effect on others.

I do my part to heal my world.

———

Society itself is an accident to the spirit and if society in any of its forms is to be justified morally, it must be justified at the bar of the individual conscience.

George Santayana

Conscious Change

Today I recognize myself for the work I have done in recovery. I have not been satisfied with half a life and half a spirit. I have visited my own inner darkness and shed light. I have faced my tiger in the night. Many times I have been told that I dig too deeply and look too hard, but I have done it anyway — done it so that I can see the sky and hear the birds. So that the day is full and rich. I have made a decision to do what I could do, both to heal myself and to break the chain of addiction and co-dependency that passes down through generations. Today I know that it has been worth the struggle — if only to see life in all its beauty for just a moment.

I am grateful for the path I have taken.

In the mouth of society are many diseased teeth, decayed to the bones of the jaws. But society makes no effort to have them extracted and be rid of the affliction; it contents itself with gold fillings.

Kahlil Gibran

Letting People In

Today I know that I never need to be alone and isolated in my life again. I have learned to let in other people because I have learned to let myself in to me. I have no more secrets from myself. No more frightening corners within that I am too terrified to look at. Because I am willing to see myself as I am, warts and all, I can let others see me as I am and in so doing, I release myself from isolation. What I thought I so carefully hid was, in fact, seen by others anyway, and it is easier for them to be with me when we do not have to play the game of being blind. Relating is not just about sharing mind space but sharing heart space as well. Today I have company.

I can let people see me.

The person who tries to live alone will not succeed as a human being. His heart withers if it does not answer another heart. His mind shrinks away if he hears only the echoes of his own thoughts and no other inspiration.

Pearl S. Buck

Frustration

I can detach from my own annoyance today. Things do not necessarily always go exactly as I would like them to. When this happens, I have a choice. I can step forward into the situation, try to control it and get it to look the way I would like it to be. Or I can step back from the situation and watch it and my reaction to it and give it some space to work itself out. Somehow, going with the flow leaves me more serene than going against it. Losing my serenity feels worse than giving up what I want in the moment. I have worked much harder for peace of mind than for some fleeting pleasure. My momentary desire might be less painful to live without than my inner equilibrium.

I can detach from my control.

Improvement makes straight roads; but the crooked roads without improvement are roads of genius.

William Blake

Today I do what it takes to get from one side of a situation to the other without losing myself and abandoning my sanity and better judgment. Acting out became a way of life with me and self-discipline a dirty word. But without some self-discipline, I create messes for myself. Eventually my self-esteem gets lowered because I am not able to negotiate situations comfortably. Today I use tools of recovery and the 12-Step program when my own feelings get difficult for me to handle. The first tool is to recognize that it is *my* feelings and reactions that are giving me the problem. I do a personal inventory first to see where I am coming from within myself before I project my feelings onto the situation.

I use the tools I have learned.

———

That is a bad bridge
which is shorter than the stream.

German proverb

Slipping

Today I will not hold myself to a tight regime of recovered behavior. If I slip or behave in ways that I am sorry for, I will promptly admit it to myself and make any amends that might help me to move on. If I slipped on the pavement, I would instinctively recover myself and continue walking as quickly as possible. I would recognize that cursing myself all the way down the block for losing my balance would be pointless and self-defeating. Life is like a walk down the block and slipping is a part of the walk. Today I will focus on the walk rather than on the slip. The voices in my head that tell me falling is more important than moving along are sick voices. I recognize that I am powerless over them, and I will turn them over and let them go.

I accept my slips and falls.

Do I contradict myself?
Very well then I contradict myself.
I am large, I contain multitudes.

Walt Whitman

Today I do not try to be unique. In my desire to be different from the crowd, I divide myself from myself. I have to create a superficial false self to conform to my vision of uniqueness while I run away from the deeper truth that under the skin we are all one. Somehow I fear that if I give in to this sense of oneness, I will lose myself. I forget that in losing myself I find myself. Holding on gives me the illusion of living the life I think I "should" be living, but life has taught me that it is in letting go that I am truly present. I rest quietly today in the recognition that there is no need to be other than who I am.

I am united with others in a deep way.

———

To be happy in this world, especially when youth is past, it is necessary to feel oneself not merely an isolated individual whose day will soon be over, but part of the stream of life flowing on from the first germ to the remote and unknown future.

Bertrand Russell

Repressed Feelings

Today I follow the path of repressed feelings into my unconscious with understanding and compassion. When I was young, I repressed feelings of anger and pain because at the time I had nowhere to go with them. They were too dangerous for me; expressing them to myself would have meant I had to lose my place in the world, the only place I had. It was a question of survival and basic security. When repressed feelings come to the surface, they feel overwhelming and frightening. There is all this feeling and no particular place to go with it. I can project it into my life today or I can follow the feeling toward its origin and see what it's really about and allow myself to re-feel or re-experience it in the safety of today.

*I understand where
my feelings come from.*

Just as courage imperils life, fear protects it.
Leonardo da Vinci

Enjoying The Ordinary

Today I embrace the ordinary. Everyday living in an orderly pleasant way has a wisdom all its own. Easy, enjoyable routine is healing. I learned while young to live from crisis to crisis, and it came to be that I only felt really alive and connected to my family when we were in turmoil. I let that go today and allow myself to trust and enjoy daily life. Absence of crisis does not have to mean bleak and boring. There is a deep beauty to everyday life, a quiet vitality that gives the world a sweet hum, something peaceful and comforting that this everyday life creates.

I love the ordinary.

———

Nothing is said now
that has not been said before.

Terence

Doing What Feels Good

Today I see that when I become obsessed
with fame and fortune or with what could
be in my life, it is because I do not love what
I do. When I love what I do, fantasies fall
away because I am living in sync with my
inner self. There is no point in doing what I
hate. My needs are not grandiose; life is not
about becoming anything, only about doing
what feels good to me. When I do what I
enjoy, I am not constantly grating against
my nervous system. There is no nobility in
forcing what I don't like on myself. Money
and fame do not fill the void that I create in
myself by doing, day after day, what leaves
me empty inside. First I need to ask myself
the question, What do I enjoy?

I am able to do what I enjoy.

---

*A celebrity is a person who works hard all
his life to become known, then wears dark
glasses to avoid being recognized.*

Fred Allen

Having My Own Life

I will have my own life today. I spent a long time taking care of other people. So long that I learned to feel safest as the person behind the scenes, competent and sustaining of others. It is good to help others but not to hold them up. Not only will they not learn to stand on their own feet, but if at some point they choose to have their own life, I will experience their moving away as a profound rejection and a sort of personal death. When I take care of everyone but myself, I die a little each day. I am in need of care and upkeep just as they are, and when I neglect myself, I neglect my life.

I will take care of my own life.

———

Living well and beautifully and
justly are all one thing.

Sophocles

The Inner Teacher

Today I realize that what I am searching so desperately for is within me. There is no teacher who is a better teacher for me than I am for myself. No one's intuition is more tuned into my heart than my own. No mind can better penetrate the depths of my being than the mind I have. Why should I spend all my time letting others tell me who I am when I can go into the quiet of my own spirit and learn it for myself? The anchor that I wish to cast out to sea so that I will not float away I will seek within. I am capable of knowing and learning what I need for happiness with my own faculties if I trust my teacher within.

I am anchored from within.

Console thyself, thou wouldst not seek me,
if thou hadst not found me.

Blaise Pascal

Inner Faith

Today I do not trust anything that I have not experienced within my own heart as true. My eyes and my senses may deceive me but there is part of me that quietly tells me what is real. For me, there is a Higher Power and Wisdom that guides my life, a loving presence that judges no one but remains as an indifferent, available energy source that I can come into contact with through inner quiet and meditation. What I hear through my ears is that life is made up of external circumstances, but what I sense through my intuition is that life is a spiritual journey — unfolding lessons — each leading me closer to purity and love.

I trust what my heart tells me.

———

*Faith consists in believing not what seems true,
but what seems false to our understanding.*

Voltaire

My Natural Healing Process

Today I notice the way that healing happens naturally for me. Sometimes I have healing dreams that seem to release negative images from my unconscious so that I can see them, feel them and let them go. While I am going through internal changes, my dreams show me what I have been holding inside, and they cleanse the storehouse of my unconscious. Tears release grief and when I am putting myself through the recovery process there will be times when I cry a lot. Though I will not necessarily know what I am doing, I will let myself weep, knowing that tears would not be coming if they were not within me to be shed. They heal me and restore a sense of health, well being and equilibrium.

I let myself have
my natural healing process.

Nature to be commanded must be obeyed.
                                        Francis Bacon

Programming My Unconscious

Today I consciously use the creative power of my mind. I have learned from the recovery process that problems which are stored in my unconscious repeat themselves in situations in my life. My unconscious repeats the experiences I need to work on, choosing just the right people with whom to work them out. Why not turn this creative patterning power to my advantage by visualizing what I would like in my life over and over again, thus sending new information to my unconscious.

I give my unconscious
positive life challenges to solve.

———

At least 10 times every day affirm, "I expect the best and with God's help will attain the best." In so doing your thoughts will run toward the best and become conditioned to its realization. This practice will bring all of your powers to focus on the attainment of the best. It will bring the best to you.

Norman Vincent Peale

Disease Of Attitudes

Today I remember that "ours is a disease of attitudes." The negative thinking and destructive attitudes that I learned growing up with addiction and dysfunction remain with me until I do something to change them. Forcing positivity on top of negativity does not work, neither side rings true when I do that. There is no quick way to correct this because a lot went into its making. What I need to do is remember that I have trouble with my attitudes and that I need special work in that area to restore them to sanity. Acknowledging the problem, sharing it out loud and turning it over helps. As I rework my past issues, I will remember that I need to make constant attitude adjustments so that I can maintain the good work that I am doing.

I recognize that my negative attitudes hamper my recovery path.

Be led by reason.

Greek proverb

Today I know that life is made up of little things. What makes or breaks the day are the small moments — what makes or breaks a life is how we live it day-to-day. It is the hardly perceptible decisions I make throughout my day that add up to how I spend my time and what it feels like. If I need to handle a situation differently, it is generally not one large decision that will mark the overall change but a thousand small ones. It is much more difficult for me to be present in the process of ordering and reordering small things than large things. It is the little decisions of the day that confound me — translating a large resolve into the many small actions that will make it real.

I show up for the small things.

Be grateful for luck.
Pay the thunder no mind —
Listen to the birds.
And don't hate nobody.

Eubie Blake

Going Within

Today I feel that the secret of life is to love the one I have. There is something to this energy of love that is transforming. Why should I wish all the time to be somebody else or to live another sort of life. My life is fine just the way it is. Why should I wish that it were different? There is life and beauty within me all of the time but I walk right by it. I avoid quiet, but it is in silence that I am able to reach deeply enough within to pull out that force of love with which I can nurture myself and those around me. I rush around as if there were somewhere more important to go than within my own heart. All that I need to be I already am. Today I will look inside.

I look within myself for myself.

One word frees us of
all the weight and pain of life:
That word is love.

Sophocles

Today I will visualize in my mind's eye good things for myself and my life. I will actually imagine that what I want in my life is already here. I will participate in my inner dream as if it were reality. I will taste it, smell it, see it and believe it. Seeing is believing and believing is seeing. There is more than enough room in life for all of us to have what we want. If good things happen for others, why not me? I will take a risk in my imagination today and envision what I would like to see in my life. I have nothing to lose by trying.

It's fun to visualize my good.

———

Beholding beauty with the eye of the mind,
he will be enabled to bring forth, not images of
beauty, but realities (for he has hold not
of an image but of a reality).

Plato

Life

I will remember today that life is to be enjoyed. I will enjoy life and my relationships. I will become willing to be a person capable of being happy. So many times I have wanted to give up on life — to crawl into a little ball and hide myself away. But life renews itself and somehow I want to come back for more. It has an undeniable sweetness and I feel that I belong here. Sometimes I have this wonderful contented feeling, almost as if life were rocking me in its arms. I have a friendly attachment to this thing called life. I can't help loving it.

I'm glad I'm here.

Life was meant to be lived, and curiosity must be kept alive. One must never, for whatever reason, turn his back on life.

Eleanor Roosevelt

Today I will be mindful of my actions. I will pay attention to everything I do with new awareness. I will be mindful in my interactions within and without. I will see what normally I would be too distracted to notice. To be mindful is to be in touch and alive, to be willing to participate in life, to be willing to be with myself. It is not enough anymore just to drag myself through time and hope for the best. There is so much just at my fingertips; all I need do is attune my mind to a peaceful frequency and see the beauty that is already there. Everywhere around me life waits to be seen and felt. Today I will not waste the opportunity to experience the life I have.

*I am full of awareness of
what lies around me.*

———

*This is the grand atonement . . .
the being in touch.*

D. H. Lawrence

Purity

Today I understand that I was born deeply dependent. It is no wonder that it was so terrifying when I stopped being able to rely on my parents — I was so completely vulnerable and needy. "Where were you when I needed you?" is the cry of my inner child. I have taken some of this cry with me into adulthood as a feeling that no one can really understand me or my pain, but as I look back it seems so obvious and uncomplicated. Of course I feel bereft and desperate — who wouldn't? It is the wall that I have built around those feelings that is so complicated and hard to dismantle. It is made of self-delusion, unspoken grief, resentment and fear. It is when I can take down my own wall, return to my former innocent state and feel what that child felt, that I can find myself and my Higher Power.

I can face the full extent of my pain.

———

Unless you become like a child
you cannot enter the kingdom of heaven.
Matthew 18:3

Today I recognize the futility of passing on old dysfunctional patterns. It is pointless to try to correct the present with methods that didn't even work in the past. I really can change and recognizing my desire to control those near to me is the beginning of that change. Now I can see myself in action — I can actually feel myself begin to get anxious, then reach for control to bring my anxiety level down. It is a great relief to myself and those around me when I am willing to live with my own powerlessness over their lives. Today when I feel an urge to control, it will be a signal to me to focus on what is going on in my own self and life.

I recognize the futility
of trying to control others.

___

Grace is given of God but
knowledge is bought in the market.
                                        Arthur Hugh Clough

119

Getting To Know Myself

Today I will cease looking for my face in the faces of other people. If I want to know who I am, I will observe myself in action; I will watch the inner workings of my mind. No one has better access to me than me. If I don't know who and what I'm about, I certainly cannot expect anyone else to tell me. When I seek to be defined by others, I live from pillar to post, from one person's idea of me, to a job description, to a title or role, to another person's idea of who I am. I lose my center and seek to find it in people, places and things outside of myself. Who I am is a changing thing. There is no one me to get to know and finally be done with it. I let myself change and grow.

I befriend my changing self.

The more peculiarly his own a man's character is, the better it fits him.

Cicero

Today I do not require anyone's testimony but my own to prove to me that my life has depth, beauty and meaning. It is in the quiet recognition of my inner spirit that I know this to be true. Each day brings forth a kind of truth if I am able to see it as such. Lessons that are mine to learn come forward into life in a variety of forms. What I am ready to learn next is in front of me. There is a kind of trust that I am developing for the actual process of living as I grow and change. There is a kind of faith in life that grows inside of me.

I accept the deep meaning of my life.

It is your own asset to yourself
and the constant voice of your own reason,
and not of others,
that should make you believe.

Blaise Pascal

Rigid Projections

I do not need to make anything other than what it is today. I have overassigned meaning to certain types of relationships, work and situations, but now I see that assigning deep meaning to my own fantasies puts limits on the object on which I project. I come to expect only what I have already decided is there, and I miss the moment-to-moment experience. My fantasies also limit me because I box myself into a predictable pattern. No matter how rich my thoughts, they become rigid and binding when they are fixed rather than spontaneous, and in so being they lose their life and their beauty.

I seize the moment as it arrives.

There is no meaning to life except the meaning man gives to his life by the unfolding of his powers, by living productively.

Erich Fromm

Today I accept the futility of carrying on a constant argument with the past. It is my responsibility to work through and release what was painful in my past and is in my way today. No matter how much I may wish certain things had been different, I have no power to change them. Once I confront my pain, shame and anger and understand them for what they are, I can extract the wisdom I gained from those experiences, reframe them in a new light and move on. There is no need to dwell on the past if I am willing to accept it as it was. Sometimes my denial of my own past and my insistence on pretending that it didn't hurt keep me caught up in it. In allowing myself to be loyal to my own truth as I saw it, I can walk up to the closed doors within my own heart and open them.

I can live with my past just as it was.

This only is denied to God: the power to undo the past.

Agathon

Change And Growth

Today I recognize that life, whether or not I want it to be, is a constant process of death and rebirth. We are always being born again into new awareness, new understanding and fresh ways of being. It is impossible to stand still; in fact, standing still is an illusion. If I am able to accept that my life is in a process of constant growth, I will be less thrown by changing circumstances around me. I will see them for what they are, a reflection of the deep pattern of growth in life. If I seek stability in sameness, I run the risk of forcing myself and those around me to conform to something we no longer are — to be what we were yesterday. My relationships are in a constantly evolving state and so am I. I will learn to seek stability within that state.

I seek my stability in
the quiet observation of change.

———

All growth is a leap in the dark, a spontaneous
unpremeditated act without benefit of experience.
                                        Henry Miller

I recognize today that I am in charge of my own learning. Life is constantly offering up circumstances that are useful in my personal growth. I can move through the situation, live it out, extract the wisdom that is in me or repeat it over and over again, exhausting myself and learning very little. The deepest and most appropriate things I need to learn in life are generally right in front of me. Life is my guru if I can use it as such. It is rich with subtle learning if I look for it. The real achievement for me today is to learn to be in my own skin, to see truth in all that surrounds me, to know that placing value and judgment is pointless and illusory — all of life is valuable.

My lessons come from my life.

———

What one knows is in youth of little moment; they know enough who know how to learn.

Henry Adams

Crisis

Today I recognize that I am not another person's crisis. In my co-dependency I have felt that the way to be close to someone is to become them. When they had a crisis, it became mine, or worse I actually entered into and became the crisis itself. By fusing with the person and the problem, I create a new problem. Wouldn't it be better if I let another person have a crisis without me? I can help perhaps by listening or lightening some burden, but I cannot help by becoming the problem — I only make everything worse. It is important for me to let another person have all of their feelings about a situation and for me to have all of my feelings about that situation, but I cannot have all of their feelings without robbing both of us of ourselves.

I am not another person's crisis.

If you can keep your head when all about you are losing theirs, it's just possible you haven't grasped the situation.

Jean Kerr

Today I see that I have been looking to other people, places and things to be my Higher Power. When I recognize that I am not those people, objects or circumstances, that there is not a piece of me alive in everything outside myself, I see who and where I really live. It is an illusion that I am alive everywhere but in myself — an illusion of co-dependency. I am alive within me, and I am one with a Higher Power who lives within me, as me, through me — and through all things. When I think I am everywhere else, I will remember that a Higher Power lives everywhere in all people and things but that my path to a Higher Power is through myself. Once I contact the Higher Power in me, I can recognize it in others and contact it there as well.

I look to my own
heart as my conduit to spirit.

———

It is the heart which
experiences God and not the reason.

Blaise Pascal

127

Appropriate Anger

Today I see that there is such a thing as appropriate anger, anger that actually works to further a situation and resolve feelings. My problem has been repressed anger and rage. I kept myself from feeling so much of my anger in the past that it stored up inside of me, and waited for opportunities to leak out in tiny ways or to blast out. I need to recognize and own the anger that I carry and look for therapeutic situations in which I can dump it once and for all. When I get rid of it in these ways, I will no longer need to get it out of my system by making big problems out of small ones or by raging at people who don't deserve it.

I look for appropriate
outlets for my anger and rage.

———

It is easy to fly into a passion — anybody can do that but to be angry with the right person to the right extent at the right time and with the right object in the right way, that is not easy, and it is not everyone who can do it.
Aristotle

Today I recognize that I am deeply connected to my past and that to hold things
against my past is to hold things against me.
I will work to resolve old hurts and anger so
that I can let it go and free myself. One of
the keys to understanding and releasing is to
know truly that people were not hurting
me intentionally. They really were operating
from what they knew at the time and what
they were aware of. Why they could not see
more was a function of many things, such as:
the times, their own pasts, the social atmosphere, what was generally understood and
so on. I have so much more available to help
me understand things and give me support
than my parents did. It must have been hard
for them to carry so much pain in silence.

I am lucky to have support.

———

*We are not free to use today or to promise
tomorrow because we are already mortgaged
to yesterday.*

Ralph Waldo Emerson

Forgiveness

Today I understand that forgiveness returns me to my original state of oneness and spirituality. True forgiveness connects me to a childlike, spontaneous state. Perhaps my forgiveness was abused as a child and put me in the painfully vulnerable position of going back for more. I do not need to worry about that today, whether or not I become soured on the idea of forgiving, it is still better for me to let go of the resentment than to hold onto it. Because I ultimately value my serenity over my desire for revenge, I see the advantage in doing what I need to do to forgive and move on, it is the best thing I can do for myself.

I release people in my mind.

———

We must develop and maintain the capacity to forgive. He who is devoid of the power to forgive is devoid of the power to love. There is some good in the worst of us and some evil in the best of us. When we discover this, we are less prone to hate our enemies.

Martin Luther King, Jr.

Today I see my tendency to become discouraged as its own entity, not necessarily connected to particular events. At some deep level I may carry the fear and thought that life is not meant to work out for me. Because I could not improve my home situation no matter how hard I tried, how desperately I wanted to or how much I changed and improved myself, I live with a quiet, unspoken sense of defeat. Even when I put on a happy-go-lucky or brave face, I am hiding these deeper feelings even from myself. There is no more reason why life should not work out for me than anyone else. The feeling of discouragement that I hold in my heart is just a feeling. I can turn it over to a higher source and ask for help.

I see my discouragement as a force of its own.

———

Trouble has no necessary connection with discouragement — discouragement has a germ of its own, as different from trouble as arthritis is different from a stiff joint.

F. Scott Fitzgerald

Changing My Life Situation

I can change my life situation. Trying and trying and trying to get something right that never seems to work is self-destructive and makes me feel like a failure. I have a right to succeed and feel good about myself. Change is one of the most difficult of life's challenges. It is perfectly all right for me to want my life to feel comfortable to me as well as manageable. I don't know what my future may hold in store for me at any given time, but I know that it is good. When I follow my heart, I align myself with my greater good and when I align myself with my greater good, things have a way of falling into place. Today I entertain the possibility that my life can work out as I might like it to.

I am able to make changes.

The absurd man is he who never changes.
August Barthélemy

Today I really see what carrying anger and rage from situations that occurred decades ago has done to me and my present life. I have dumped not anger but rage from early wounds on those who surround me today and have seen them as responsible for that pain. When I am really willing to look at the depth of the wounds that I carry from living in a dysfunctional home, I can begin to let the past go. It is different from feeling sorry for myself to admit the full extent of my hurt and fear of abandonment. It is giving myself a chance to live in today by seeing yesterday, not as I wish it had been but how it was for me, understanding that no one meant for it to be that way; it just happened.

I see my hurt for what it was.

If you are distressed by anything external, the pain is not due to the thing itself but to your own estimate of it; and this you have the power to revoke at any moment.

Marcus Aurelius

Doing Our Best

One of the gifts of recovery today is that in really admitting to the full extent of the dysfunction, pain and abandonment in my home I see that it was unintentional. No one meant for things to get as bad as they got; they got that way because no one could do otherwise. If people in my past had known better, they would have done better. I see how much recovery has changed me. I would not handle situations today the way I did a few years ago. I was doing the best I was capable of and so were they. My parents had a past too, and if they had learned perfect habits, I'm sure they would have passed them on to me. They gave me what they had, just as I do my children. We are all doing our best with what we are aware of.

We are doing the best we can.

———

This is Daddy's bedtime secret for today: Man is born broken. He lives by mending. The grace of God is glue.

Eugene O'Neill

Today I let myself have my angry feelings without letting them have me. In the past because anger was a complete no-no, I learned to stuff my own anger so that even I no longer knew what I was feeling. This cost me a great deal in relating to the world because natural anger is meant to protect me from harm and help me to know how I feel. I lost track of my own responses to situations because I denied my feelings before I knew I had them. Sometimes just to let myself know that I am angry is enough. I needn't let the feeling flood me or make me feel I need to react. My anger also can just be information for me, having little to do with anyone else. It can simply let me know that something is not okay so that I can be honest with myself and with others and can stay with what is really going on.

I let my anger inform me.

---

*He who has been
angry becomes cool again.*

Greek proverb

Connecting Through The Positive

Today I am no longer willing to sweat the small stuff. Years of working through each detail of my life, of making everything important and full of meaning, have taught me that it's just too intense and burdensome to live that way. I drive myself crazy doing this, as well as those around me. I know now that living without taking other people's inventories is the calmest, easiest way to get through my day. I also realize keeping the focus on myself does not necessarily mean that I have to think about myself all day. I have proven to myself that life has a way of working out if I let it. There are really only a few times in life when real crises occur. When I create crisis in order to feel alive, I experience only a very temporary electrical jolt. I can feel connected today through meditation and the gift of insight. I can experience love.

I connect through direct
experience, meditation and love.

———

If you be not ill, be not ill-like.

Scottish proverb

Today I see that the only real point of power is in the present, which is to say that life cannot be lived backward or forward but only in the context of today. If I truly let myself have this moment and all that it contains, I will experience more in the way of enlightenment than if I become a brilliant student of the past or a psychic who can predict the future. It is in the present moment that all the waters meet and all the wisdom of the ages lies; it is the now that calls me to it with open arms. I work out my past, not because it is right or good or proper, but because it allows me to be in fuller possession of my present. By releasing and returning to me those parts of me that remain prisoner in my own psychic and emotional jail, I can have access to them now.

I allow myself this moment.

Real generosity toward the
future lies in giving all to the present.

Albert Camus

Dreams

Today I pay attention to the contents of my dreams and listen to what they are trying to tell me. The unconscious is a marvelous thing, and my own unconscious speaks to me while I am asleep and my defenses are down. It uses the language of myth and symbol to show me the truth that it contains. I carry things that affect me, but it is difficult for me to see or know what I am holding inside. My dreams attempt to show me in a masked form what these things are. That way, if I am ready to know them, I will, and if not, I need not. My dreams are my unconscious talking to me.

I respect the content of my dreams.

———

We are not hypocrites in our sleep.
William Hazlitt

Today I know that there is nothing to be afraid of because my Higher Power and love underpin all that is. At the very core of me is not darkness and fear but love and light. My mind is constantly creating fears to hold on to, not because I am afraid to admit to the extent of my hatred, but because I am afraid to admit to the extent of my love. When I allow myself to be at the source of love and to recognize it as a fundamental mystery of creation, I sense that no matter what happens I will be all right.

I allow love to be the basis of my life.

You must love all that God has created, both his entire world and each single tiny sand grain of it. Love each tiny leaf, each beam of sunshine. You must love the animals, love every plant. If you love all things, you will also attain the divine mystery that is in all things. For then your ability to perceive the truth will grow every day, and your mind will open itself to an all-embracing love.

Fyodor Dostoyevski

Being With Life

Today I allow myself just to be with life. Somehow it doesn't have to prove anything to me or give me any more than I already have to be okay. The lessons I have learned through pain and loneliness have taught me that I can survive my most difficult feelings and still come home to a place of love and acceptance. Life is always renewing itself; nothing lasts, good or bad, and that is just the way it is. It is enough today to enjoy my coffee, to take a walk, to appreciate the people in my life. I can rest in a quiet sort of understanding that this is what it's all about; all the searching turned up such an ordinary but beautiful thing.

I am enraptured with the ordinary.

We are all, it seems, saving ourselves for the Senior Prom. But many of us forget that somewhere along the line we must learn to dance.

Alan Harrington

Today I accept that recovery has changed my baseline of experience. When I release trauma, terror and rage, they are really gone. I used to have those emotions on top, and they could surface and apply themselves to any situation. Psychodramatically and therapeutically, I have blown them out of my system, and through sharing, my pain has been lifted. I need no longer carry inside of me what is gone. I can operate from a different place. It really is possible to live my life without all that baggage. It has been an immense amount of work, but it has been more than worth it. I am enjoying my freedom from the past that had me in its grip.

I am operating differently today.

———

To remain young one must change. The perpetual campus hero is not a young man but an old boy.

Alexander Chase

Character

I will rely on my basic strength and knowing today. All the theories in the world cannot make up a "me" if there is no "me" inside. I cannot replace ideas and methods for a self. Part of my co-dependency seeks for self-definition through the ideas and thoughts of others. This leaves me a sitting duck for being led and manipulated by anyone who shows an interest in me. Even though co-dependency makes me feel as if I am without a self, it is not really so. I have simply mislaid myself in other people's pockets or hidden what self I had underneath layers and layers of protection. Recovery helps me to remove those layers so that I can see better what was always there.

I have self and character.

———

When a person lacks character,
he is badly in need of a method.

Albert Camus

Today I make choices about my company and friends. Whom I choose to spend time with is very important to me, and the relationships that I begin I wish to respect and nurture. A handful of dear friends is far more meaningful to me than lots of acquaintances. I choose to share myself where I feel a return. I want both to have a friend and to be a friend. One of the unusual gifts of growing up in a dysfunctional household was that I learned the value of friendship because I had to turn to my friends to meet very deep needs. I am grateful for what I learned and felt from and with my friends.

I value friendship.

———

A friend to everybody
and to nobody is the same thing.

Spanish proverb

Letting Go Of Perfectionism

May 23

Today I will not demand that my life be perfect in order for me to love it nor will I demand that all of my relationships be perfect for me to value and respect them. If I try to make my life and relationships perfect, I will be constantly engaged in a neurotic battle with my transitory illusion of perfection. There is no such thing as an ideal and to insist that life be ideal is to miss the forest for the trees. I will not condemn myself to the constant feeling that I have drawn the short straw because perfection is in the eyes of the beholder — it is subjective. I will not ask the moment to be more than the moment — I will not be conditional in my love.

I see perfection
in things as they are.

———

A good garden may have some weeds.
                                        Thomas Fuller

Beauty and Immortality

Today I sense that a part of me is immortal and is somehow connected with life eternal. How could I know what I know or feel what I feel if a Higher Presence were not within me? The eyes that look in on me and those out of which I see, in a way, are the same eyes. I feel no separation on this level — I feel one with all things. I am sure that this part of me could never die, though my body does. In my mind it does not seem natural not to extend into infinity. I see my higher life as eternal and changeless.

I am an immortal being.

Our Creator would never have made such lovely days, and have given us the deep hearts to enjoy them, unless we were meant to be immortal.

Nathaniel Hawthorne

Leaving Abuse Behind

Today I see my life as my life. If I do not take care of it, make plans and dream dreams, who will? I am not second in my own heart — there has to be a place on this earth where I come first so that the little baby inside of me feels loved and held. I will come first with me. In the same way that I will protect my children from harm I will protect myself. Abuse is a part of a dysfunctional family system. I hardly saw it as abuse — it was just what was, a painful way of life — the only one I knew. I do not need to recreate abusive situations in my life today in order to feel stable or as if I have a home.

I can leave an abusive situation.

———

Every area of trouble gives out a ray of hope and the one unchangeable certainty is that nothing is certain or unchangeable.
John F. Kennedy

Today I do not accept other people's truth as my truth. Even if what they believe seems more right than what I believe or better or more obvious, I need to give myself credit for feeling and seeing what I feel and see. Learning is meaningful to me as it relates to or is understood within the working of my own mind. Without something in me making it relevant, learning is very disconnected. I am the learner behind the information; I am the seer behind the seen. I learn by direct experience. I learn to trust the perceptions that I gain from my own observation of life.

I learn for myself.

> *Never believe on faith.*
> *See for yourself!*
> *What you yourself don't learn,*
> *You don't know.*

Bertolt Brecht

Inner Newness

I am new inside today. I feel pink and tender as if young tissue were growing within. I have been willing to take an ultimate risk by looking at the state of my life and insides, not as I wish they were, but as they actually are. I have experienced an inner death. I have walked through spaces inside my mind and heart that felt life-threatening, and I have felt the terror of full honesty. What I did not expect was this sense of birth and newness. Somehow life feels full of possibility for new and different experiences. I thought that I would be stuck in anger and blame forever, but I see today that I did not need to feel so down on myself for feeling those feelings. They are just a part of the process.

I accept my feelings
whether or not I like them.

———

Growth is the only evidence of life.
John Henry Newman

Today I accept my feelings of anger and blame without beating myself up for them. Feelings aren't facts; they are meant to inform me of what is going on inside of me. When I constantly judge myself for what I feel, I make my difficult emotions much more complicated and they last ten times as long. There is nothing inherently wrong with any feelings — so what if I am angry and feel like getting mad? Accepting this allows the feeling to pass through me. Fighting it keeps me tangled up inside with no way out. Judging myself doesn't help anyone, least of all me. Frightening feelings are just frightening feelings. I do not have to overreact to them.

My own feelings need
not toss me in every direction.

———

No man is angry that feels not himself hurt.
Francis Bacon

Healing

Sometimes healing doesn't feel good. Sometimes it involves deep pain. The effect of healing is gentle, free and wonderful, but the road leading to it can be hellish. Now I understand that the Psalms were referring to a spiritual enlightenment involving a death and a rebirth. In order to be born into enlightenment it is necessary that I face and clear out the dark and scary parts of myself. I need all of me for a life of spiritual freedom. Today I know that I was never alone along the way and that I need never feel alone again.

My Higher Power has always been with me.

———

Keep your sense of wonder. I suggest that you maintain that sense of wonder and that feeling of discovery because, speaking as a "hard-nosed businessman," it is also the road to success, because that is what fuels the fires of imagination. That is what powers your perseverance and inspires the creativity which the business world lacks in abundance.

Paul Woolard

Today I will pray for a miracle in a situation that seems too much for me to handle or understand. There are times that I just don't have what it takes to work a situation out. I'm too loaded up with fears and anxieties. What could it hurt to pray for a little divine guidance or intervention? At the least it will help to lift my burden and at best it will aid in a genuine shift in perception that might truly help my situation. When I feel stuck and as if I have explored every option and am still nowhere, I will pray for a miracle.

*I allow my consciousness
to reach out into the unknown
and ask for help.*

———

A miracle is a shift in perception and prayer is the medium of miracles.

from *A Course In Miracles*

Fear Of Change

Today I am able to live with my fear that I will not like myself or those close to me if we change. Change is threatening and recovery includes change. It doesn't matter to my fearful self if the change is for the better or worse. In fact, change for the better can sometimes be even more threatening. I fear that I will not know how to act or have the tools to be with the "better" without smearing my disease all over it. I remind myself today, again, that I do not have to grow perfectly. This is not an easy road but the gains are so apparent that I will have faith that my tough times will come to an end.

It's okay that I fear the outcome of change in myself and my relationships.

The felt unreliability of human experience brought about by the inhuman acceleration of historical change has led every sensitive modern mind to the recording of some kind of nausea, of intellectual vertigo.

Susan Sontag

Emotional Growth

*T*oday I accept that growth is emotional detoxification and as such is messy. No wonder my life can smell bad when I am going through these experiences. When I get near to the experience of real love, it brings up everything that is not love in an attempt to clear it out. During this process, I get very down on myself because I feel that I'm not really growing, but it is just these powerful feelings of rage, resentment and hurt that tell me that inner change is taking place. I am healing my wounded self so that I can experience more fully a life of love and freedom.

**I can live with
some mess along the way.**

It is great to be great, but it is greater to be human.

Will Rogers

Ego Death

When I begin to experience real love, I go through an ego death. On my road to spiritual freedom, which is nothing more than learning to love, I go through what has long been called a dark night of the soul. This is a death of the ego, not in the Freudian sense, but in the way ego is defined in Eastern philosophy. I have a small *i* and a large *I*, and part of my path toward expansion into my larger external self, which is of God and Love, is a death of my smaller self, which sees the world as here only to feed my needs. Really it is through the recognition of giving and receiving and of loving that we become full.

I allow and understand
my ego death.

It is through giving that
we receive and it is through dying
that we are born to eternal life.

St. Francis of Assisi

Today I recognize my essential wholeness. While I see myself as deficient and look to others to complete me, I condemn myself to a life of reactivity. In this mode I can only spend my days trying to bend myself into the shape that I feel will make me lovable to someone else, and if they love me, I will feel both momentarily full and terrified that the feeling will go away. I will see them as in charge of my feeling loved, and I will go about using massive control maneuvers and manipulations to keep my supply on tap. If they do not love me, I will feel belittled and furious at having compromised myself to no avail. The only solution is to seek wholeness within.

I look within for love.

It is very foolish to wish to be exclusively wise.

La Rochefoucauld

Separation

❧ Today I see that some of my anger toward my parents or their generation is about my need to separate from them and seek an individual identity. Even if my parents were wonderful, it would still be natural to pick them apart in an attempt not to be like them — to put distance in the relationship. Healthy parents have an easier time allowing this process because they have their own identity and intuitively understand what their children are doing. Less healthy parents take separation as a personal indictment and tend either to hold on tighter or to reject the relationships altogether. It is difficult to separate under these circumstances because it becomes so threatening. It is difficult to establish an individual identity without fearing either great loss or engulfment.

I see separation for what it is.

We have to hate our immediate predecessors to get free of their authority.

D. H. Lawrence

I Am Not Alone

Today I know that I can do anything I need to do with God's help. When I feel alone or shaken up, I can ask for help within myself and know that it is there. Each of us is ultimately alone. Each of us has to learn our own lessons, that is what we are here to do. We can't learn anyone else's lessons for them and learning our own is difficult enough. To plow through my own psyche and face the insecurity and wounds that are there is all that I can handle. To try to live other people's lives for them is to separate myself from God because my first access to God is through and within me.

I ask for help in learning
what I need to learn.

One on God's side is a majority.
                                            Wendell Phillips

Our Own Good

Today I accept that I do not always know what is best for me. There are times when I am completely confused about what to do for myself and for those around me because I cannot see how my own issues are surfacing and coloring my present. These are the days that I need to pray and to understand that my prayers are heard. I never whisper to God that I am not heard. Prayer is my medium for change and growth. It is with me all of the time and there is no moment when I cannot elevate my consciousness and conscious contact through it. It is my way of talking to my higher self and turning over my lower self to the loving, compassionate care of a Higher Power.

I trust in my own good.

Our will is always for our own good but we do not always see what that is.

Jean-Jacques Rousseau

Today I see that honesty in my relationships does not necessarily mean that I share all the thoughts in my mind or feelings in my heart. Honesty is the place I come from and the person I most need to be square with is myself. There are times when it is destructive to a relationship to talk too much or to share each and every detail. Sometimes quiet companionship is more nourishing and healing than describing and explaining. Intimacy is not about talking; it is about being. When I share personal details of my life, I am not necessarily being intimate in the total sense. Intimacy is a willingness and an ability to be with someone with all that this entails. Talking can create a false sense of intimacy if I am not willing to do more.

I pick and choose what I share.

To refrain from imitation is the best revenge.
Marcus Aurelius

Vitality

Today I see that I needn't figure everything out. Much of life is simply meant to be lived and loosely understood. Reasoning and analyzing can be defenses against fear and anxiety. It may have helped me in the past to sort out what was going on but that was largely because what was going on was not healthy. I needed to understand that, in order not to feel crazy. When life gets healthier, figuring it all out can, in itself, become dysfunctional. It is like turning up the idle in a car when it stands still. When life goes well, I can just drive and let go of the obsession to sort out each and every detail.

I can live and trust my own vitality.

Nature drives with a loose rein and vitality of any sort can blunder through many a predicament in which reason would despair.

George Santayana

Today I will be patient with myself. When I do not do so well as I wish I would, I will not make that a reason to get down on myself. I will instead recognize that the fastest way to bring myself out of a painful funk is through understanding and being good to myself. I get caught in my own cycle of shame, resentment and blame. If a child is upset, I comfort it because I understand that that is what will make things better. Calling a child names will increase its hurt and shame. I will not call myself names either. Rather, I will show love and patience in every way I can.

I am patient with myself.

———

Patience accomplishes its object,
while hurry speeds to its ruin.

Sa'di

Idealized Selves

Today I will not create an idealized self either for me or for those I am close to. Growing up with fear and denial, I created "idealized" parents to comfort myself. I was afraid that if I saw them as being out of control and in pain I would feel like dying or disappearing. I still do that with people I love and with myself. If anyone, including myself, falls short of my ideals, I am enraged and want to toss them out of my life. We are all just human, and human is all we have to offer. When I let go of my need to create perfect images, I find that I and those I love are not so bad after all.

I can live with myself a day at a time.

When smashing monuments, save the pedestals — they always come in handy.

Stanislaw Lee

Today I will calm myself down. I accept that I can get very anxious, particularly throughout my process of recovery. When I touch the dark and frightening psychic pockets of my past, I disturb the waters of my unconscious. Though I know that I will eventually feel better and be cleaner inside, during the process I live through deep anxiety and night terrors. Feeling, understanding and articulating painful emotions rather than acting them out is new behavior. I will take extra good care of myself when I feel flooded with feelings. I will do things that make me feel good and get extra rest and good food.

*I care about myself so
I coddle myself when I need it.*

———

Worries go down better with soup than without.

Yiddish proverb

Fear

Today I allow myself to experience my fears as fears and not dictate or color my life circumstances because of them. They are real and it is understandable that I have them. Recovery mobilizes my deep fears and they come up more intensely than ever. This is a part of my process of growth and growth is not neat and tidy. When I am very afraid, I will comfort myself or seek comfort from someone else. I will understand that I am afraid and that even though I fear the worst, the worst will not necessarily happen. My feelings feel very powerful inside of me, particularly when they have been repressed and are surfacing after many years, but they are not facts. I can survive my fears and understand that they will pass.

***I have compassion
for the fearful part of me.***

———

*When men are ruled by fear, they strive to
prevent the very changes that will abate it.*

Alan Paton

Today I recognize the source of light and wisdom within me. When I look outside of myself to learn about what is actually inside, I need to exercise great discernment because some of what I see fits and some does not. There is a fountain within me that is ever full and waiting to be discovered. When I can rest quietly in this inner place, I experience a sense of fullness, and my desire to go outside diminishes and gives way to a preference for undisturbed peace. Solitude takes on a different meaning when I can contact that quiet within, life softens and external things become less important. I look for this place within me on a daily basis.

I search within.

When you have shut your doors and darkened your room, remember, never to say that you are alone; for you are not alone, but God is within, and your genius is within.

Epictetus

Truth

June 14

Today I accept that without truth there is nothing. Truth is the soil out of which sustenance grows to nourish us so that we can move in healthy directions. Lies have no food value and starve my spirit, but truth, as painful as it is sometimes, has a way of hoeing and tilling itself so that some new growth can come. Even though knowing the truth seems unnecessary or too much to carry — I know it anyway at some level. To bring truth out into the open gives it a chance to lift the veil of secrecy that has made it feel like a beast within and lets it transform into something usable that can again nurture health and life.

I am willing to live with truth.

Truth is the strong compost in which beauty may sometimes germinate.

Christopher Morley

Today I will not hide my pain and suffering from myself or from my Higher Power. When I bring my most honest and pure self to the fore and understand my essential powerlessness over situations, when I am truly willing to turn over this angst to a power greater than myself, something changes. I let go and create space for a shift in perception. I experience a quiet awakening in my life, and forces that did not have room to enter come to heal. It is in letting go that I have a chance of achieving what I desire in my life. Holding on pushes away what I want, while releasing lets it all have enough breathing room so it can stay alive.

I open my heart to my Higher Power.

Do not hide suffering from his sight,
but bring it gladly to him.

from *A Course In Miracles*

Separate Selves

Today I love you because I am willing to let you go. Before you were mine, your eyes, your hair, your voice and possessions all felt a part of me as though, in a way, I owned them. But now I know I will never own you. People don't belong to other people. You belong to life and so do I. Each day we have together is a choice. Each day I understand you are free and I am grateful that you wish to share your life with me. Because we are committed to a relationship together does not mean that you owe me your self. Your self belongs to you and mine to me. I honor your need and right to grow and change and I honor mine to do the same. I am your partner on a journey.

Each of us is our own being.

———

That is why it is important to understand the meaning of death and perhaps to find that death has great significance, great relationship with love, when you end attachment completely, then love is.

J. Krishnamurti

Today I see that having my own life begins inside of me. It is not just a function of what I do, but the attitude with which I move through my day. Having my own life is about checking in with myself to see how I'm doing. It's wearing a sweater if I'm cold and taking a break if I'm tired. It's making sure that I'm having enough fun in my life, paying attention to what I enjoy doing and doing more of that and finding ways of reducing what doesn't feel good. Having a life is letting myself have my own unique likes and dislikes and acting on them in constructive ways. It is not organizing my life so that it is good enough for everyone else, forgetting that it needs to be good enough for me.

I am with myself on the inside.

———

Every true man, sir, who is a little above the level of the beasts and plants, does not live for the sake of living without knowing how to live: but he lives so as to give a meaning and a value to his own life.

Luigi Pirandello

Changing Relationships

Today I will give myself the chance to have new kinds of relationships. The patterns set up in my youth of being either overly close or very distant are those I bring with me into adulthood. I think of intimacy as a superbonded state in which another person and I like the same things and agree on everything. Today I know that this is not intimacy. It is an experience a child may have with a parent, a feeling that someone else is completely tuned in to you, but it is not a realistic expectation in adult relationships. Disagreeing and learning to accept differences are a part of intimacy too. Distance is a part of closeness. Giving, a part of receiving. People are different from one another. Genuine trust and understanding make room for moving apart and coming together again.

I can experiment with different types
of intimate relationships.

———

To really know someone is to have loved and hated him in turn.

Marcel Jouhandeau

Today I recognize that winning is an illusion. Interpersonal relationships are not about winning and losing and neither is life. When I have a disagreement in a personal relationship and approach the solution with a competitive attitude, I may win the battle but lose the war. This is a dysfunctional habit from my past — the idea that someone has to come out on top, that someone is right and the other person is wrong. There are two or more people involved, and we each have our own point of view. If one of us has to be right, then the other has to feel beaten. Neither position will do anything to restore comfortable relating. What I really desire in my heart is to get along, and the way to do that is to give what I would like to receive both to myself and to someone else.

I realize that I cannot have
everything just as I want it.

When the passions become masters, they are vices.

Blaise Pascal

Fear Of Repeating The Past

June 20

Because my family of origin became sick, it is not fair of me to ask my family to be perfect to correct my past or to make it right. My family today is just my family today. If I try to make sure everything is perfect all the time in order to keep history from repeating itself, I will set up a new kind of problem and be overly threatened when things don't go well. It is vitally important that I let my family today be who we are and not hold us hostage to my fears of what could happen. What happened in my past need not happen again — we are different people in a different time; it is just not the same.

My family today is different
from my family of origin.

Respect the past in the full measure of its deserts, but do not make the mistake of confusing it with the present nor seek in it the ideals of the future.

José Ingenieros

Today I understand that recovery is many little acts and subtle changes in attitudes. Recovery is not talking differently — it is being different. I will follow through on plans that I make and keep my life simple. I will not allow abuse in my home, of me or anyone else. I will take a positive attitude toward my life. Recovery is not only about reworking my past — it is also about not repeating it. It is the little steps I actually take that count. Major changes can be deceptive because wherever I go, I take myself with me. A small inner change, if it is real, can have a more transforming effect than a large outer one. Setting impossible, unreachable goals for myself is just another way to stay sick. Doing something small well will give me self-respect and serenity.

Today I do only what I can do.

Our health is our sound relation to external objects; our sympathy with external being.
Ralph Waldo Emerson

Focusing On The Negative

Today I allow myself not to be perfect. No matter how well I do something, it seems to be my habit to focus on what was not perfect. Rather than enjoy what I did well and learn from what was less successful, I ignore my successes and ruminate over my mistakes. I see them as large failures and feel a deep sort of shame that is completely out of sync with the reality of the situation. Focusing on the negative and forgetting about the positive are habits that have become ingrained in the way I assess myself. I will slowly and compassionately lift myself out of this negative pattern, gently reminding myself that it is all right to enjoy the good in my life. To enjoy what is good is wise and right.

I am able to take in the positive.

———

Say "I love you" to those you love. The eternal silence is long enough to be silent in and that awaits us all.

George Eliot

Today I give with both hands. I have thought that everything needed to be negotiated, that I was being co-dependent if I gave with no thought of what I would receive in return. Now I see that giving for its own sake is the spiritual way and actually releases the gift. When I give with one hand and take with the other, I give only half of what I have and receive only half of what might be given to me. I limit myself in two ways. Somehow the universe responds to clear intention. When I fully release a gift, it goes to where it is supposed to go and what returns to me comes when and how it is right.

I am able to give fully.

There is sublime thieving in all giving.
Someone gives us all he has and we are his.
Eric Hoffer

Hesitation

Today I will walk the walk and talk the talk. It will not be good for me, ultimately, to half commit myself. In a way the particular path that I take is less significant than that I take a path. I can second guess myself and my decisions forever, but when I do, I leave myself feeling nowhere and inadequate. Because I worry about failing, I hold myself back from trying, but there is really much more to learn and grow from in trying and failing than in staying stuck. When I constantly hesitate, perhaps there are some feelings that I don't want to feel or things about myself that I am afraid to see. I will stay with that feeling of hesitancy and see where it takes me.

I am able to move.

———

He became an infidel
hesitating between two mosques.

Turkish proverb

Personal Truth

Today I know that no one from my past needs to see things the way I do for me to get better and move on. Trying to convince family members of what I have learned through my own journey can be an exercise in futility and delay my progress. First of all, each of us has our own truth that is unique unto itself. Second, we are all at different levels of understanding and acceptance of who and where we are in life. Each member of my family had different experiences. That I thought they somehow matched up was an illusion. We each experienced our childhoods in our own way and have a right to our own perceptions. I do not have to get anyone to see it my way in order for me to feel comfortable. My truth is my truth, theirs is theirs.

> *I honor my own experience*
> *and personal truth.*

If you add to the truth, you subtract from it.
The Talmud

Simplifying My Life

Today I see that I do not need to gulp life whole in order to taste it. More is not necessarily better. An alcoholic builds up a tolerance for liquor so that it takes an increasingly greater amount just to feel high. If I am grabbing at life in this way, needing to do more and more in order to get a feeling of pleasure, it is time for me to simplify. More activity, money, trips, lessons and so on are not the answer. That hole inside of me that I am trying to fill is not satisfied in this manner; overfeeding it only increases its capacity — starving it makes it shut down. When I can simplify and regulate my life so that I can really experience it as it is happening, I will have enough. I will experience my own spontaneity and creativity in the course of living my day.

I will simplify my life.

Creativity is a gift. It doesn't come through if the air is cluttered.

John Lennon

Today I understand that life is relationship and relationship is nature's stimulus for growth. Intimacy with another person demands more of me than any other experience. It calls me to stretch and grow where it hurts the most. The people with whom I choose to be intimate are selected by me through a complicated unconscious process that lifts them out of hundreds of possibilities. At some deep level, I look for a person who can, by being a sort of mirror, help me to resolve my deepest childhood wounds. I choose them not only to be close to but also to be my teacher, and they do the same with me. It is the bond between us and the unconscious knowledge that I am meant to learn from this person that help me through this very painful process of personal growth.

I grow in my intimate relationships.

And throughout all eternity I forgive you,
you forgive me.

William Blake

Dreaming Dreams

Today I will dream dreams. There is nothing wrong with having a couple of dreams for myself if they are realistic and don't remove me from life too much. To work toward a dream can be a constructive use of my talents and energies. It can give me a positive focus. If my dreams are wild and I am not willing to do the work necessary to realize them, they will only frustrate me and lower my self-esteem. If, however, I am able to dream what makes sense for me and work to put it within my reach, it can be a real process of growth and challenge. My energy and enthusiasm can help me to move through blocks and my commitment can show me that love and effort can be their own reward.

I can stretch myself.

———

You got to have a dream
If you don't have a dream
How you gonna have a dream come true?
Oscar Hammerstein, *South Pacific*

Today I will have fun. What's the point of all the work I do in recovery if my life doesn't become lighter and happier? Even though I am working through deep issues, there is no reason why I can't have some enjoyment in the process. Fun is when I relax and let things happen — when I can laugh at myself and other people — when I don't take everything in life so seriously. It is when I can enjoy a seemingly meaningless conversation just for its own sake. Fun is when it doesn't have to be all my way — when the heavy load is removed, when my meter is turned off and I just goof around in the moment. Fun is something I don't have enough of for a number of silly reasons. Today I see that there is no reason not to enjoy myself.

I can let go and have fun.

On with the dance, let joy be unconfined is my motto, whether there's any dance to dance or any joy to unconfine.

Mark Twain

Letting Go

Today I finally recognize that the only things that I have a chance of keeping are those I am willing to let go of. There is something about the way the world works in this — the tighter I hold on, the less I have. When things change, I experience feelings of abandonment. Those feelings are so real for me that I start to hold on. The tighter I hold on, the more others push me away because my energy becomes suffocating and the more they push me away, the tighter I hold on because I am in such fear of feeling abandoned again. Today, though, I will let go and live my own life, trusting through love rather than fear.

I release that which I hold.

> *Love that is hoarded*
> *Molds at last*
> *Until we know someday*
> *The only thing*
> *We ever have*
> *Is what we give away.*
>
> Edna St. Vincent Millay

Minding My Own Business

*T*oday I will mind my own business. Interfering in other people's lives doesn't help them or me. Sometimes I get fascinated by another person's problems as a way of getting away from my own insides. Sometimes I am actually seduced or excited by trouble and crisis. This is an old pattern and can only get me into trouble as a recovered person. I will be honest with myself today about my motivation for getting involved with someone else's turmoil. Is it coming from a place of caring and genuine concern or is my radar just out for a sticky situation in which to lose myself or take a vacation from my own insides? I will look within to see if I am repeating a "go-for-the-crisis" behavior pattern or simply being helpful.

I will take a personal inventory.

———

And whatsoever else shall hap tonight,
Give it an understanding, but not tongue.
William Shakespeare

Spiritual Transformation

Today I see that to change my life I have to change myself. Nothing less than a spiritual transformation will allow me to experience my current life as an alive, serene and whole person. When I say that I would like world peace, first I will understand that without inner peace there will be no world peace. One of the ways in which I can serve the cause of humanity is to be, within myself, a genuinely spiritual person — related to no sect or creed, but standing on my own as a conduit of higher truth, recognizing that each person has equal access to that knowledge. I will look for truth today within myself rather than outside. I will not wait for peace to be handed to me as some sort of prize for good behavior but will do the inner work needed to achieve it.

I seek truth within myself.

No matter how big or soft or warm your bed is, you still have to get out of it.

Grace Slick

Today I will release the shame that has a hold on my heart. When I allow a sort of historical shame of who I am to engulf me, nothing in life seems sweet or good anymore. Embarrassment is over something I do; shame is over who I am. In dysfunctional homes we feel isolated in our pain as if no one understands us. We feel that somehow we don't know how to be happy like other people do. Because our insides were ignored, we learned to shut them down and to pretend they didn't matter. We developed a persona and presented that to the world in lieu of ourselves. Relationships became increasingly hollow because less and less of who we really were came through the mask. Recovery is about removing the mask and allowing more of who we really are to come through.

I let go of debilitating shame.

You must pay for your sins. If you have already paid, please ignore this notice.

Sam Levenson

Being Enough

Today I will not tear myself up inside when I am not all that I wish to be. Somewhere along the way I internalized the message that good enough meant perfect. Everywhere society and the media say that happiness belongs to those who have it all together, who behave in a flawless manner, who are faultless. It creates the feeling in me that I have no right to feel good about myself unless I am constantly on top of things and have in my life what society feels I should have. But I know now that this isn't how it works. Feeling good about myself is an inside job. I can give myself another chance every day. I can release the negativity I am carrying around within me and fill in the empty space with self-acceptance. I can quiet my internal wars and let peace come.

I can create good feelings within me.

Be noble-minded! Our own heart, and not other men's opinions of us, forms our true honor.
Friedrich von Schiller

Today I feel open to whatever is going on, recognizing that it is the quickest way to process repressed material, the fastest way to grow and the most fun way to live my life and feel alive. In recovery I process years, even decades of material in a condensed time. There are moments when I feel like a time traveler through my own interior space. It's okay, I won't go anywhere I can't handle. Facing my insides is my ultimate spiritual challenge. I will not be hard on myself for not all at once achieving and holding my desired result. Growth is messy. I am unearthing and clearing all that is in my way. I am cleaning house, cleansing my soul. This is a process.

I will appreciate
and be patient with myself.

———

But play no tricks upon thy soul, O man;
Let fact be fact, and life the thing it can.

Arthur Hugh Clough

Pleasing Others

Today I will not be about pleasing others. This does not mean that I will adopt a defensive attitude or create myself in opposition to another. What it does mean is that I will check in with myself first so that I know what I am feeling and what I wish to do. I may have to postpone my desire or adjust for the sake of fairness or convenience. Still it is important for me to know what I am feeling so that I stay in touch with who I am. It is when I give myself away first that I get into trouble. Compromise is the stuff of relationships and life, but when I am not honest about where I am, I either go along with someone else in a mindless way and resent them later or try to manipulate and control from underneath to get what I want. I will look inside to see what is happening there.

I let myself know
what I am thinking.

———

Don't shake hands too eagerly.

Greek proverb

Today I will build on my own strengths; my days of copying are over. When I try to make myself like other people, it never works. When I give myself away by trying to be someone who will interest others, I lose my own center. Other people's authority can be a powerful drug. It's a great temptation either to placate or to challenge it. Neither need be done. Being myself is my greatest defense against falling prey either to the desire to *become* other people or to take them on in a contest of wills. Staying with who I am and risking feeling alone will ultimately be more help to me than trying to align myself with others for my security.

I can be myself.

———

Never do what a specialist can do better. Discover your own specialty. Do not despair if your specialty appears to be more delicate, a lesser thing. Make up in finesse what you lose in force.

Jean Cocteau

Character Defects

Today I remember that when a negative characteristic is on its way out of myself it seems worse than ever. I see it everywhere as it falls out of control. This seems to be part of the process of working its way out of my system — that it shows up in an intense way in my life. Just as a rash appears on my skin when something is moving through my system, the characteristic that is leaving my psyche or internal system appears like a rash in my behavior and personality. This can be discouraging because what I want most to let go of appears to be all over but I will remind myself that the deeper the problem, the more intense its working out process. I humbly ask God or the Higher Power to remove this defect of character and trust that it will be so.

I turn over a character defect.

Who overcomes by force
hath overcome but half his foe.

John Milton

Dealing With Shame

Today I will remember that Rome was not built in a day, and I will not be all that I wish to be overnight. When I act in ways that I later feel shame about, I will remind myself that to feel shame and release it is healthy — to get lost in it will get me into trouble. When I hold onto shame, I run the risk that I will eventually resent the feeling and look for other people to pin it on or to blame. Or in order to release the pain of feeling ashamed myself, I may act it out by shaming someone else. Today when I feel shame, I will remember that no one is perfect and that I need not be either. I make prompt amends to anyone I may hurt, including myself, and move on in my day.

**I am capable
of moving past shame.**

———

The deeper the sorrow, the less tongue it hath.

The Talmud

191

Experiencing Higher Power

July 10

Today I understand that truth is an experience rather than a thought. While I conceive of a Higher Power as a form or an entity, I remove myself from the experience of a Higher Power. I can pose the questions and live the life that would move me progressively closer to oneness or equanimity, but I will only reap the full benefit when I can actually "be still and know." I will feel and know the presence of a Higher Power. Rather than creating the thought, I will create stillness and quiet and allow a feeling of peace, quiet, exhilaration and well-being to come over me.

> **I experience *truth*
> rather than think about it.**

The function of the intellect consists in leading the mind to a higher field of consciousness by proposing all sorts of questions which are beyond itself. The mystery is solved by living it, by seeing into its working, by actually experiencing the significance of life.

D. T. Suzuki

Today I respect the need for ritual in my life. Reunions with old friends and family that mark time and help me to realize that I care about others and am cared about by them are deeply important. To understand that life has seasons, that they change and flow into one another, each looking different but retaining a kind of connection helps me to remember that I am on a journey. That life is meant to be lived and understood and appreciated. Rituals help me to make transitions. They show me how far I have come and where I need to go. They allow me a structure through which to celebrate life and grieve loss. They provide me with an opening into the world of experience through using their structure as a gateway.

I am open to organizing and being a part of important events.

You have your brush, you have your colors, you paint paradise, then in you go.

Nikos Kazantzakis

Living With Variables

Today I recognize the wisdom of seeing and feeling the good in my life. Nothing in life is permanent. What feels good today will pass, but that need not prevent me from enjoying and appreciating it. In the past I experienced a loss of safety and protection and that was traumatic. In an effort to keep myself from that kind of pain I remain hypervigilant. Anything that feels too good I cut in half, and what looks threatening I double, imagining all possible negative scenarios in the hopes of outwitting and avoiding the circumstances of my life. The truth is that I will always have an easy full side to my life along with a problematic side; they run alongside one another. This is normal and natural. I can learn to live with both.

I can live with contradiction.

Observe always that everything is the result of change and get used to thinking that there is nothing Nature loves so well as to change existing forms and make new ones like them.

Marcus Aurelius

Today I realize that part of maturity is to accept that I cannot necessarily have everything just the way I want it. The thought that I should be able to act out everything in adulthood that I wasn't able to as a child just doesn't work. When children's needs go unmet, they carry into adulthood a desire to have all of their needs catered to. This is the stuff of co-dependent, problematic relationships. To be aware of one's needs is what is important. From this intelligence, mature decisions can be made. Because I am aware of my needs does not necessarily mean that someone else has to meet them or that I have a right to expect them to. Negating another person's presence will do nothing to enhance my own.

I am ready to grow up.

When I was a child, I spoke as a child, I understood as a child, I thought as a child: but when I became a man, I put away childish things.

1 Corinthians 13:11

Fear

Today I will not give my power away to someone else by being afraid of them. When I obsess in fearful ways about another person, I systematically remove strength and self-assuredness from myself. I imagine all sorts of ways this person might reject or judge me; I see them as harboring negative feelings toward me. I give this person the power to tell me how I feel about myself. I do this so regularly, in so many little ways, that I am hardly aware that I am doing it. I define myself according to other people's opinions of me. I remind myself today that I am in this life to learn my own lessons, not to turn myself inside out in an effort to get other people's approval.

I allow myself not to be afraid of others.

———

But if men who do not see life would only approach nearer to the phantoms which alarm them, and would examine them, they would perceive that for them also they are only phantoms and not realities.

Leo Tolstoy

Unique Vision

Today I will see what I see. It is in allowing myself my own unique perspective that I gain a sort of individualized point of view to operate from. Just because others don't share my vision of a thing doesn't make it wrong. In fact, sometimes it is when I am willing to follow through on my own perception or solution that I make my greatest contribution to myself and others. I take pleasure in my own point of view. It's fun and it gives a congruency to my life when I live from my inside to my outside. Today I am willing to allow that flow to take place. I see that the things I do and surround myself with are metaphors for what goes on inside of me. I have fun being me.

I let the artist in me see out.

———

There is a natural hootchy-kootchy motion to a goldfish.

Walt Disney

My Natural Size

Today I accept my gifts and talents. I have kept myself in a sort of fog about my assets to avoid feeling guilty, competitive or overly responsible for them. Though I have craved attention and validation, when I actually receive it, what comes up for me is shame and anxiety. I worry that if I stand out too much in any direction, good or bad, I will become an easy target. I realize now that I can feel those feelings, move through them and let them go. I need not stay locked in fear. When I am willing to accept both my strengths and my limitations, I feel better about my life — I create a safe space for myself.

I accept my natural size.

———

It is very necessary that a man should be appraised early in life that it is a masquerade in which he finds himself. For otherwise there are many things which he will fail to understand.

Arthur Schopenhauer

My Feelings Of Abandonment

Today I am willing to feel my feelings of abandonment rather than run away from them. When my abandonment fears get triggered, I am thrown into deep anxiety and I hold on to anything around me as if for dear life. I want the feelings to go away, and I mistakenly think that if I keep all of those people, places and things I need exactly where I want them, everything will work out. But life is change and people change. There is no way to keep anything where I want it all the time. My anchor needs to be within myself. If I allow myself to experience my deep feelings of abandonment rather than run from them, I have a chance of working through them.

I can tolerate feeling alone.

———

Yea, though I walk through the
valley of the shadow of death, I will fear
no evil, for thou art with me.

Psalm 23:4

Laughter

Today I remember that the catharsis of laughter can be just as powerful and transforming as the catharsis of tears or anger. To laugh with my entire being — to really get the joke and the joy of it all — is an unforgettable experience, one that leaves me forever a little different. Laughter is a symphony to the soul, and those we truly laugh with become special kinds of friends. When I cannot laugh, I cannot be. It means that I am so rigidly locked within myself that no air can get in. When I laugh, everything sort of loosens up inside, flies around and settles back down in an easier place. I remind myself that it is important to cry and equally so to laugh.

I feel the importance of
laughter in my life.

No man who has once heartily and wholly
laughed can be altogether irreclaimably bad.

Thomas Carlyle

What I Can Do

Today I will focus on what I can do rather than on what I cannot do. I have never been able to get anywhere in life by saying I can't do something. When I feel a wall going up in front of me, I will remember that every wall has a hole. I will find that hole — that way to create an opening. I know that success in my life has come from saying "I can" and "I will," from taking action rather than sitting on the sidelines of my own ambitions and dreams. Failure is part of success. If I try to fail over and over again, I will also try to succeed as many times. The only real failure is not to try. Today I will assume that if I really want to do something, there is a way that I can do it. I will look at the possibilities rather than spend my precious time analyzing over and over again all the liabilities.

I will move forward in
a positive direction.

Talk doesn't cook rice.

Chinese proverb

Accepting Mood Swings

Today I will not be down on myself if I seem to swing in my moods through my recovery process. Mood swings have been scary to me, so I use them as a way to judge (or misjudge) my health. I force myself to be in a stable good mood and then I feel I'm okay. As I re-experience old, repressed feelings, it is possible that I will feel deeply disoriented, angry, rageful or depressed and then two hours later almost high. This is not just because I can't control my moods — I am opening myself to all that is going on with me — I am no longer denying parts of myself so that I will fit into a designated constellation of roles. I am allowing what is happening with me to happen.

I understand that my moods might swing in this life-changing process.

———

Just trust yourself, then you will know how to live.

Johann Wolfgang von Goethe

Today I will remember that all of the change I am going through is stressful and that I need to take particularly good care of myself in these recovery months or years. I will get extra rest. Inner growth at this accelerated rate is exhausting, and I need more rest and sleep than usual. I will simplify my life and make my day manageable, letting go of what does not really need to be accomplished and doing the basics. I need time to process the changes taking place inside of me, empty, quiet time just to watch the clouds float by. I will do things that feel particularly good to me whatever they are, and I will eat well and exercise. These are challenging days, so I'll learn to be good to myself.

I fill my tank before I empty it.

———

Do not make yourself low; people will tread on your head.

Yiddish proverb

Despair

Today I will not run away from despair. The dark night of the soul comes before the dawn. I am not here only to feel good and to take life easy. Despair in recovery can mean that I am letting go of old ways of coping and trying to learn new ones. I am here to grow and to experience myself as a spiritual being connected on some mysterious level to all of life. If I deny myself my greatest pain, I will keep myself from my deepest joy. There is a divine order in what appears to be chaos. There is method in the madness. There will be lessons and quiet miracles, freedom from inner bondage and calm after turbulence. All that I go through has a purpose if I choose to look at it that way. I trust that even though I cannot always see it, the universe is unfolding as it should.

I trust that there is a plan for me.

———

You may not know it but at the far end of despair is a white clearing where one is almost happy.

Jean Anouilh

Learning From Love

Today I see through love anything is possible. When I look through the compassionate and powerful eyes of love, I see a different world, a different person. Love teaches me to see what is beneath the surface, what is hidden to my eye but known by my heart. I will not deny love's wisdom today. I will let it be and work its magic in my life. I will give it freely to others whether they know what I am doing or not. Why should I judge myself or anyone else? Love does not judge, not because it is wrong to do so, but because love is a complete feeling and doesn't need to look at other things. It seeks to heal rather than to wound. Love is life and God and my Higher Self.

I can love.

———

Who so loves
Believes the impossible.
Elizabeth Barrett Browning

Self-Cleansing

Today I understand that I am cleaning my channel for living. For me to allow my higher self to come through me requires that my being is as clear and free of debris as possible. Held resentment, rage, fear and depression are the debris of my spirit. They keep me from my greater good. The energy it takes to manage and hold these powerful feelings in, so that they will not come shooting out inappropriately, is energy drawn out of my spirit. It creates a fuel deficit for day-to-day living so that I feel exhausted rather than energized. The storehouse of my unconscious is a busy, burdened place when I ask it to hold rather than process.

I clean my insides to free myself.

I had to set limits to knowledge in order to make a place for faith.

Immanuel Kant

Today I realize that it is through letting go that I am able to keep my life in order, trusting that something beyond me holds my life together. In my relationships letting go seems crucial. When I try to hold on and control my intimate relationships, I strangle the life out of them, and the very safety I wish to insure gets lost because people feel controlled by me and want to get away. The tighter I hold on, the more I send out signals of mistrust and fear and I begin to create that around me. When I am able to release my grip on people close to me, what binds the relationship on a deeper level can come into play and begin to work. Though I cannot see it, it is a stronger bond.

I will let go in my
intimate relationships.

Every good thought you think is contributing its share to the ultimate result of your life.
Grenville Kleiser

Controlling Others

I will show up for my life today. What matters is not the result of my day but that I lived it. When I try to live in the result rather than in the process, I force myself and others to conform to my idea of what things should be like. I lose my ability to let the day happen in my attempt to get it to look a particular way. I cannot possibly foresee all of the variables that will enter my day before they enter it, and when I overcontrol, I leave out the potential for those who play a role. I also leave no room for my Higher Power or chance to work when I insist on a preconceived format. It is good to be able to make plans for myself, but when I catch myself trying to control others within it, I will check in to see what's going on with me at a deeper level.

I can let go of control of others.

———

Change your thoughts and you change your world.

Norman Vincent Peale

Sitting With My Own Insides

Today I know that I cannot control others. If I want to make anything better or different for those close to me, the person to work on is myself. If I begin here, the rest has a better chance of falling into place. I keep my own act clean. Next comes the relationship. If I know where I am, I can send out clear messages. I will not burden the relationship by asking it to perform in such a way as to alleviate my own anxiety and fill up an empty hole inside of me. To try to get into someone else's skin and control them from their inside is intrusive and destructive. It removes their autonomy and self-respect, hampers their growth and forces them to be constantly second-guessing themselves. It also relieves me of the duty and responsibility of sitting with my own insides because I am sitting in someone else's.

I sit with my own insides and allow those close to me to sit with theirs.

We think in generalities, we live in detail.
Alfred North Whitehead

Special Care

Today I understand that as I move through a process of recovery I am taking a journey through my unconscious. I have chosen to feel my feelings rather than act them out in ways that have become destructive for me. I have become willing to visit the dark corners of my mind and see what is there. If I were traveling through rugged territory I would expect to be both exhilarated and tired. Today I see that recovery is sort of being outward bound within my own mind, and I need to keep myself in good shape with extra rest, good food and quiet time. If I am tired, it is for a good reason. I will listen to myself with love and care.

I take special care
of myself in recovery.

———

Nothing great is created suddenly, any more than a bunch of grapes or a fig. If you tell me that you desire a fig, I answer you that there must be time. Let it first blossom, then bear fruit, then ripen.

Epictetus

My Shadow Self

Today I honor myself for being able to confront my own shadow. My willingness to do this has tremendous potential for transforming my life. What I keep in darkness and hold as a secret from myself and others within my psyche has a strong hold over me. It takes a lot of psychic energy to hold secrets in place, to keep them from leaking out into the vision of others, to keep them only half known to myself. I have to hide my secrets in darkness, which means keeping parts of my psyche in a sort of shadowy, murky, lightless space. The pain of knowing is sharp, sometimes excruciating, but then it is over. The pain of not knowing is a constant nagging ache. I choose to know today.

I am able to fill
my mind with light.

———

You're as sick as your secrets.

12-Step saying

Characterological Change

Today I remind myself that recovery is a process and that it takes time. In the beginning things seemed to improve almost immediately. I felt a great sense of relief and pieces fell into place that had previously made no sense. Then as I continued to confront deep and painful issues from my past, things seemed to get worse. My life felt as if it were falling apart. And there were many times that my loneliness and desperation were very close to the surface. After that I experienced change. It wasn't always comfortable, and sometimes I resented it, but all in all I feel different and different feels better. Today if I feel out of sorts, I know it is because out of sorts is no longer the norm.

I feel change in my life.

———

First it gets better, then it gets worse, then it gets different.

12-Step slogan

Today I understand that when I go deep into myself — into old pain and anger — and access the fouled feelings that have been stored on my insides, I am reaching into a wounded and diseased area and am doing surgery in my emotional body. When I release these feelings therapeutically, I am draining toxin and infection out of my body. This is as dramatic to my being as any kind of surgery and is potentially as life-saving. I will care for myself in a special and tender way. If I am drained and a little sore inside, I will understand that I have undergone a curative procedure and I will give myself the time I need to recover.

*I understand what
emotional surgery entails.*

Sanity is very rare; [everyone] has a dash of madness.

Ralph Waldo Emerson.

My Own Center

*T*oday I am not a different person with each person I interact. I have my own center. In my co-dependency I responded so much to others' perceptions that I was actually different according to what I perceived to be their individual expectations. While a little bit of this is natural, I was experiencing a loss of self and an intrusion of a false self that left me feeling overly vulnerable and at other people's mercy. As I have regained my center, I have a more consistent inner self, and my self-respect remains intact. I feel whole and centered as I move through my life with my own insides, instead of mine and everybody else's.

I have a center inside.

———

For my thoughts
are not your thoughts,
neither are your ways my ways.

Isaiah 55:8

Today I notice that I am in touch with my feelings very quickly. I know what I think and feel almost immediately. What used to take me days now takes seconds, and I find that I give much more weight to what I feel than what someone else says. I used to ask other people to tell me what I felt. Now I tell other people what I feel. Life makes much more sense when I live it from the inside out rather than the outside in. My personality seems so much more focused and in view, while at the same time less rigid and increasingly flexible and spontaneous. This feels like a gift of recovery.

*I know what goes on
inside of me.*

I am more afraid of my own heart than of the Pope and all his Cardinals. I have within me the great Pope, self.

Martin Luther

New Learning

Today I will learn something new. I will open my mind to new ways of looking at the same old thing. I will intervene in my habitual, hypnotic patterns of thought that keep me doing the same thing over and over again. I will recognize that if I am going to feel truly alive I need to bring my renewed self to each day. Research has proven that new approaches to learning actually cause brain growth. When I take a fresh look at old material or learn something new, I actually grow new brain cells. This is what keeps my brain like the brain of a young person. Though my body will grow old, my brain can stay young and flexible through new learning. This will affect my whole life.

I can learn each day.

———

Anyone who stops learning is old, whether at twenty or eighty. Anyone who keeps learning stays young. The greatest thing in life is to keep your mind young.

Henry Ford

Fear

Today I will honor my little feelings of fear when they arise. Fear was planted into the animal side of our nature to protect us, and that type of fear can still alert me to potential danger. My fear can tell me that something is not good for me at the moment. I get into trouble, however, when I judge things and decide that because they aren't good for me, they aren't good for anyone and there is something wrong about them. I also need to remember to keep an open mind so that I can discern if the fear is helping me take care of myself or is holding me back in a world of hesitation and judgment. I will look at both possibilities.

I can look at my fear.

There are times when fear is good.
It must keep its watchful place
At the heart's controls.
There is advantage in the wisdom
Won from pain.

Aeschylus

Love

Today I remember that all things remain in love. That love is my greatest teacher and my closest friend. Love is the one emotion that always has the power to restore my inner balance. When I am closed to love, I keep myself in a state of anxiety; when I can open a corner of my heart and let love in, things change. It is as if a strong ray of light were shining in a darkened room and shedding light. Things begin to look different — less threatening, more understandable. Love is available to me at all times, not only when I have an object of love. I can love just for its own sake because it opens me up inside and makes me feel better about moving into my day. I do not need to tell or show anyone that I feel this — it can just be a quiet contentment inside of me.

I can let love enter.

Love is nature's second sun.
George Chapman

Today I do not regret past losses. Loss is an inevitable part of life, and generally I find that loss contains a hidden gain. In order for change to happen there must be loss, but it is only part of the process. If I can accept it gracefully and see that it might be part of the overall scheme of things, it will be easier to move from it on to something else. Part of letting loss go is to let myself grieve, to allow the painful feelings attached to what I have lost have their full play. Even if it makes me feel weak or unable to cope, it will keep the healing process moving if I do not get stuck in resisting the pain of loss. Then I can release and make room for other things to enter my life.

I can grieve my losses.

———

You must lose a fly to catch a trout.
George Herbert

Separating Past From Present

Today I can take care of myself in the present. I can identify feelings as they come up and separate them — those that belong to the past and those that belong to the present. If they belong to the past, I will not make them about my life today but instead will understand that something current has triggered them. The enormity of my response is probably not about what is going on right now. If I make it about my present, my life will quickly feel overwhelming and unmanageable. I will seek help from people and situations that are designed to assist me, and I will separate what is about today from what belongs to yesterday.

*I do not make my
present about my past.*

———

*Deliver thyself as a roe from the hand of
the hunter, and as a bird from the hand of the
fowler.*

Proverbs 6:5

Living With My Highest Good

Today I recognize the beauty that is me and mine. I have majesty at my fingertips. I have wisdom, grace and love. I reach high, higher, higher toward my divine godlike nature. I no longer separate myself from my Higher Power — I am thine and thou art mine, use me as thy instrument. There is no need to run away; there is nowhere to run. I am coming home to my best nature, to my greatest good. When I deny my higher self, I deny God, and when I deny God, I deny my higher self because we are one in the same.

I live with the best in me.

What a piece of work is man! . . .
In action how like an angel!
In apprehension how like a God!
The beauty of the world!
The paragon of animals!

William Shakespeare

Stages Of Life

Each stage of life has gains and losses that are an inherent part of change. Each time I move to a new stage, I suffer the partial or total loss of the old. The loss is as real as the gain and I need to feel them both. If I refuse to experience the loss, I will have trouble fully entering into and enjoying the gain. If I want to really grow, I will need to accept what accompanies growth. My fear of abandonment and chaos has made change feel threatening. It has taught me to try to hang on to everything I love so that it will never go away. But life doesn't happen that way. I need to let go and move out of the way and let life happen if I want to be happy.

I can let change happen.

———

It is the image in the mind that binds us to our lost treasures, but it is the loss that shapes the image.

Colette

Today I can process painful feelings without falling apart or projecting them onto someone else. When I go through my own painful feelings by blaming them on others, I miss my own lessons. I will own what is mine and leave it for someone else to own what is theirs. If I am willing to do my part, then perhaps a power greater than me can restore my sanity, which gets temporarily mislaid when current situations trigger painful, unresolved emotions from my past. It is amazing how much power my feelings have when my past gets mixed with my present. I feel flooded, overwhelmed and confused. It will take time but I am capable of feeling them and understanding them if I want to.

*I can sort out
confusing feelings.*

———

The past is the present, isn't it? It's the future, too. We all tried to lie out of that but life won't let us.

Eugene O'Neill

Those Special People

Today I recognize that there are people in my life through whom God works, whose tenderness of heart and love of life and humanity make them part of a fleet of divine messengers. They are people who, in some mysterious way, are there when my need is greatest and help me to save my own life and the lives of those I love. I understand that this is a gift that I repay by giving it to someone else. Because giving at this level is done with such love and awareness, the givers are being nourished by their very act of giving. Their channel is open; they are receiving and giving simultaneously. I thank these people with all my heart. I am inspired by their generosity because I know, firsthand, how much it means.

I rest in prayer and gratitude.

———

True eloquence makes light of eloquence, true morality makes light of morality.

Blaise Pascal

Emotional Boil

Today I will not jump over my wounds to forgive too soon. It is necessary for me to live with my feelings as they are. When I deny deep pain and anger and push myself to forgive, I keep that pain and anger from ever being healed. I will go into my feelings as they are and give them all the space they need to mushroom, to have their moment, to live inside of me without my beating them to death. Whether or not my feelings are reasonable or good or nice, they are there. Denying them only keeps them alive in a turgid state. Today I let my emotional infection boil up and then in its own time drain and heal.

*I let my feelings run
their course.*

Never does the human soul appear so strong as when it foregoes revenge and dares forgive an injury.

E. H. Chapin

Real Feelings

Today when I feel extreme anxiety, I will ask myself what feelings I am not allowing myself to feel. Am I in an anxious state because I am afraid of sitting with anger or fear? When my entire body is racked with anxiety, what is really going on with me — what feelings am I refusing to experience, what truth am I denying? I remind myself today that I will get farther faster if I allow myself to know fully what is going on with me. Skirting around or denying parts of myself gets me nowhere; it postpones any healing or resolution and makes my feelings come out sideways in hurtful and confusing ways. I will move into rather than away from what is happening inside of me. I will let myself be free inside.

I stay with my real feelings.

———

Life is a series of experiences, each one of which makes us bigger, even though sometimes it is hard to realize this.

Henry Ford

Processing Painful Feelings

Today when something upsets me, I allow myself to have my feelings about it. There is no need to legislate the outcome before I know what is contained in the present. I can handle what life brings to me if I am able to know what I feel because that is how I learn what I do and do not like, what suits me and what does not. My feelings help me to know who I am. I get over painful situations infinitely more quickly when I allow myself to have the feelings that are mobilized around them. As I do this, the questions are answered and the mystery clears up. Feeling my feelings is a process. It takes hours sometimes. It can be tiring but it is ultimately the shortest way out of a painful place.

I let myself have my feelings.

Assimilate every mistake without dwelling on it. By all means, you should do whatever you can to get off your own back.

Richard M. Swinn

Having A Happy Relationship

Today I will think positive thoughts about my ability to have a healthy, intimate relationship. I have felt a lack of models in this area, coupled with my own disillusionment over relationships that didn't work out. This need not make me feel that I cannot have satisfying relationships in my life today. Instead of repeating what didn't work, I will try to learn from them and see if I can do things differently. If I feel myself beating my head against a wall doing the same old things over and over again, with the same unsatisfactory results, I will try something different. Life is really an experiment and there is always room for positive change.

I can live in a happy relationship.

Nothing in the world is single,
All things by a law divine
In one spirit meet and mingle.

Percy Shelley

228

Today I realize that truth and beauty are at one with a Higher Power. There is so much more beauty in this world than I am able to take in. There are skies and meadows, oceans and rugged hills, animals, birds and people. Truth is everywhere in the symmetry of nature, in the perfection of a sunset. Truth waits for me in the depths of my unconscious to be discovered. It is there beneath the chatter and distractions of any given moment when I can sit and be with it.

*I am a part of eternal
truth and beauty.*

———

*When old age shall this generation waste.
They shalt remain in midst of other
Woe than ours a friend to man
To whom thou sayest
Beauty is truth, truth beauty
That's all ye know on earth
And all ye need to know.*

John Keats

Jealousy

Today I can allow a feeling to flower. As Krishnamurti says, it is nature's way to let all living things flower, then die out, so why not jealousy? If the truth in a situation is that I am jealous, to pretend otherwise to myself puts my insides in a state of chaos and conflict. Why not let the full feeling emerge, flower and die out? Holding it in will serve no purpose except to confuse the issue and keep the feeling alive in a semidormant state. I need not act on jealousy but I can know it is there, move into it, explore it and understand it. Fully letting the emotion have its moment and giving it some breathing room in my consciousness allow it to come and go rather than stay lodged within me.

I allow emotions to flower fully.

———

Jealousy is beautiful only on a young and ardent face. After the first wrinkles, trust must return.

Alfred Capus

Where Am I In Nature?

Today I accept my true place in the nature of things. I am neither nothing nor am I everything. I am a connecting link between the earth and the heavens. I have the natures of both a beast and a saint. I am capable of greatness or meanness. I am all of this, wide and deep. There is nowhere for me to journey but to push against the limits of my own knowing, my own soul. No tomorrow promises greater gains than yesterday — it all connects through me, in the here and now, the only real point of power, the intersection from which I can move wherever I choose to move.

I am a part of earth and heaven.

For in fact what is man in nature? A nothing in comparison with the Infinite and All in comparison with Nothing, a mean between nothing and everything.

Blaise Pascal

Having My Feelings

Today I can have all of my feelings around a painful situation. I still catch myself trying to edit out my most annoying and difficult responses or the ones I feel I shouldn't have. In so doing I feel an undercurrent of unresolved conflict churning around my insides. When I let them out one by one, look at them, feel them and have them, they disappear. It is when I keep them in an unfelt, hidden state that they have such power within me. Having all of my feelings around a situation is what allows me to move through it. Acting them out in an attempt not to feel them is what keeps me stuck. I used to think expressing feelings was having them, but today I understand that the first step is simply to feel them fully.

I am able to have my feelings.

———

There are many truths of which the full meaning cannot be realized until personal experience has brought it home.

John Stuart Mill

Today I can allow a Higher Power to play an active and a practical role in my life. When I let go, I begin a chain reaction within my psyche. It is as if one thought form is connected with another, so when I make a small beginning by releasing my grip on one thought, person, place or situation, it reverberates throughout my consciousness. I am connected up inside of myself to many levels — spiritual, mental and physical. I am also affected by and affect the consciousness of those people around me. What I do to release myself cannot help but create space for others to follow if they so choose. Just a small act of letting go can bear fruit in areas yet unseen by me. I trust. I allow myself to reach up.

I can ask for
and receive help.

Let go and let God.

12-Step saying

Change In Relationships

Today I will dare to imagine that relationships in my life really can change. Because there has been deep hurt in a relationship, it does not mean that I must forfeit that person. Things can change — life is always changing — why not relationships? I am amazed at the extent to which I have transformed my insides through recovery. I really feel like a different person in my emotions and my ability to live my life in a sane and peaceful way. Anything that has been sick can get better, and if two people want a relationship to change and are willing to work on it and allow growth to take place, it can transform and take new shape.

I can allow my
relationships to get better.

———

A man that studieth revenge keeps his own wounds green, which otherwise would heal and do well.

Francis Bacon

Today I see that my life is full of choices. I also see that it is not so much what I do with my life that adds up inside of me but how I do it. My life is in my hands to live as I choose to live it. I seek a balance between self-determined action and respect for God's timetable. I understand that forcing something is out of tune with the natural flow of life but that does not mean I should not make choices and take actions. To allow for life and the universe to work, I will take an action, let go of the results and trust that if my desire is right for me it will manifest. Just as a tree does not seek to pick its own fruits, I can turn over my results and release my preoccupied hold on them. I can make friends with life on its own terms and live by its natural laws.

*I choose to live
with my eyes open.*

Arrange whatever pieces come your way.
Virginia Woolf

Came To Believe

Today I really believe I do not need to
solve all of my problems in life alone. When
I become willing to see things in a different
way, miracles happen. If I insist on my point
of view and make no room for anything else,
I am painting myself into a corner that I will
have trouble getting out of. There is no problem that my Higher Power and I cannot
meet together. I will use the second step in
all my affairs that feel unmanageable. I can
come to believe that a power greater than
myself can restore any area of my life to
sanity, a painful relationship, a dysfunctional
situation, a crisis — anytime I feel that the
walls are closing in on me, I can turn to this
step and use it, over and over and over
again.

*I am not alone in meeting
life's challenges.*

———

*Came to believe that a power greater than
myself could restore me to sanity.*
Step 2, Alcoholics Anonymous

Today I allow my vulnerability to show. I have walked a long road, as everyone has. I have gained a tremendous sense of self-respect for my willingness to meet the challenges of recovery — to meet my inner depths. I have learned that my greatest chance to meet my life with my insides intact is to remain vulnerable — to remain alive. I do not need to hide my real self from others anymore in order to keep from feeling pain. I can let myself show, and in this way I get the support I need and so desire. I no longer push away that which I want the most.

I can be vulnerable.

———

To be loved at first sight, a man should have at the same time something to respect and something to pity in his face.

Stendahl

Isolation

Today I will not isolate myself with my feelings. Part of living with my newfound health means that I no longer isolate myself. When I send out "don't-come-near-me" messages, no one does come near me. Then I feel more alone and further isolated. I will not get my needs met unless I am willing to risk letting them show or speaking them out with other people. When I open my heart to trusted people, I get more of what I really want, and I am surprised at how often people identify with me. Life is not a piece of cake for anyone, so why should I pretend or even desire to get through without having the edges show once in a while?

I can let others in.

———

People are crying up at the rich and variegated plumage of the peacock, and he is himself blushing at the sight of his ugly feet.

Sa'di

Today I accept that each time I grow or change, somewhere pain will be present. I have greatly accelerated my growth process in recovery. Issues that I may have accumulated over a period of decades I am dealing with in a much shorter time frame. The pain of confronting myself in these ways will be present alongside the joy that I feel. The easiest way to have the joy rests in not denying the pain, which is also a natural part of the process. All change requires a giving up, and this in itself is cause for mourning. It is this giving up, however, that clears the path for change. I know today that I am going through a purification process and though it is not easy, it is deeply worthwhile.

*I can accept the pain
that accompanies change.*

———

In order to unify in ourselves or unite with others, we must change, renounce, give ourselves; and this violence to ourselves partakes of pain.

Pierre Teilhard de Chardin

Boundaries

Today forgiveness is a practical thing and I put it to work in my relationships. When I forgive, it doesn't mean that I give myself away; rather it affords me the opportunity to see where I am holding resentments so I can understand better where I need boundaries. Forgiving gives me a chance to begin to let things change — there are no guarantees. What I need to keep in mind is that boundaries keep me sane. Restoring a relationship to health does not mean that I become the sacrifice. Perhaps sanity means less closeness. Even if I give up moments of what seemed like intimacy, I protect myself from the fallout that happens when we can't sustain the intensity of that intimacy.

I can have boundaries
where they feel good to me.

Forgive your enemies but never forget their names.

Edward I. Koch

240

Forgiveness And Anger

Today I see that I cannot really forgive while I am holding on to anger. I try for forgiveness because I know that ultimately it will give me freedom but when I come near to it, what comes up for me is anger. My rage is deeper than my ability to forgive. That is all I have today. Part of my healing is to know this. It is the rage that built up in me being a child ignored in my own home with no one to go to for protection, my anger at having reversed roles with my parents and at having to be their parent. How burdened I felt carrying their painful emotions for them because they were unable to own them. I lived with the hurt because they "felt fine" and could not feel their own feelings. I will process these feelings now and leave the rest in the hands of my Higher Power.

I am where I am and it's okay.

It is easier to forgive an enemy than a friend.
Madame Dorothée Deluzy

Independence And Autonomy

Today I understand the meaning and feeling of boundaries. Boundaries are set in childhood with parents. Children gradually push parents away, a little at a time, as they can tolerate the space and independence. Each time they gain more control over their own beings, they experience themselves differently. When children are not allowed to push their parents away because the parents can't tolerate being separate, children are not able to establish their boundaries. When parents do not allow their children to push them away and move out of their sphere of control, they are telling their children that they can't live without them and the children feel guilty establishing their own independence.

*I have a right and
a need for independence.*

———

*Individualism is rather like innocence; there
must be something unconscious about it.*

Louis Kronenberger

Self-Knowledge

Today I know that I understand others to the degree that I understand myself. It is through my search for self-knowledge that I learn what I need to know to get along with another person. It is through looking inward that I come to perceive what is around me. My quiet observation and willingness to look at myself through clear and impartial eyes create a window through which I can see both inside and outside. The person I need to understand is me. I am sort of a blueprint for all people, and when I am willing to know who I am, I also have a chance of knowing who other people are.

I will look inside.

Know thyself.

Socrates

Calming Down

I can let myself calm down when I am
upset. When I am stirred up inside and my
emotions are very agitated, life looks different to me than when I am not. When I was
growing up, I repressed my feelings because
I had nowhere to go with them. Because that
was true yesterday, it does not mean that
today I have to over-react to each and every
feeling I have so as not to fall into the same
trap. When I am wrought up inside, it is
okay to let myself just calm down and relax
and know that when I have done this, things
will look different. Rash action happens
when I can't stay with and feel my feelings.
The actual experience of feeling makes me
so uncomfortable that I act out.

I can let myself calm down.

---

*Often the test of courage is not to die but
to live.*

Conte Vittorio Alfieri

244

Self-Perception

*T*oday I know when I am anxious or in pain. The reason that I know this is because (1) I am no longer stuffing my anxiety so that I can't feel it or anything else and (2) I am not constantly living with a low level of discomfort. When anxiety comes up for me, it feels different, and I am out of sorts. I can see this as a gift today. It is wonderful that I am on intimate enough terms with my insides to know what is going on with them and that I feel good enough about myself to let myself actually have my feelings without acting out on them. I have someone to take care of me today and that is me. When I am not myself, I check in to find out why. When I find out, I take steps to solve it or get some comfort.

I have my own insides.

---

*All great discoveries
are made by men whose feelings
run ahead of their thinking.*

C. H. Parkhurst

Living With The Good

Today I place myself on the side of the positive forces within me. There are parts of me that want love in my life and parts of me that do not. I am ready to walk with the parts of me that do. I know enough about life to have observed by now that I can see what is good and loving or what is wrong. Aligning myself with my own positive forces does not require that I adopt an attitude of denial about what is negative. Denial only keeps pain frozen in place. I can know both good and bad are there and actively choose to live in the good most of the time.

I can live the good life.

———

Man is fond of counting his troubles but he does not count his joys. If he counted them up as he ought to, he would see that every lot has enough happiness provided for it.

Fyodor Dostoyevski

Today I can allow myself to feel normal. The deep reservoir of pain and the intense feeling of a lack of safety that I carried around inside of me made me feel separate from other people. It gave me the feeling of being different, of watching the rest of the world through a dusty glass. In recovery I have reached into the black hole inside me, released the tight mass of pain and allowed breath, air and sunlight to return. I am no longer carrying the internal pressure I once had that kept me from myself and the life around me. I have moved through my own internal space and have come to know that there is nothing there I cannot handle with the help of spiritual faith.

It's time to be normal.

———

It is not irritating to be where one is. It is only irritating to think one would like to be somewhere else.

John Cage

Being Hurt

Today if I feel hurt by someone, I can give myself time to process my response before I make it worse by over-reacting. Staying with my hurt feelings and exploring them will get me much farther than blowing up. I will learn something about my own vulnerabilities and I will see where my limits are. I can tell someone I am hurt without feeling the relationship has to end. I can take some space if I need it and give myself time to get over my hurt feelings. I can forgive myself for not being able to hear just anything and know that I have a right to be self-protective. I can see someone else as just a person, too, and forgive them for being insensitive, knowing that I am also insensitive at times. I can hold on to my hurt for a while but then I can and will let it go.

I can handle being hurt.

———

When the heart is full, the eyes overflow.
Sholem Aleichem

Independence From The Mother

Today I understand that maturity and taking responsibility for myself begin early in
childhood. Each thing I learned to do for
myself as a child taught me that I could take
care of myself. My dependence on my mother physically had the power both to sustain
my life and to crush my spirit. The illusion
of childhood was that, because I depended
on someone for my physical needs, I needed
that person emotionally as well. This is not
true. My emotional needs can and should be
met from a variety of sources. This is how I
learn that I can live, survive and be happy in
the world. Emotional independence from my
mother is a deep need that enables me to
lead a full emotional life of my own.

I can survive on my own.

———

*Grown up, and that is a terribly hard
thing to do. It is much easier to skip it and go
from one childhood to another.*

F. Scott Fitzgerald

Living With My Feelings

I do not have to forgive anyone today because it is the right or kind thing to do. That type of forgiveness cheats me and the other person. I will not forgive because I feel guilty for my anger or because I want to keep someone in my life. If I really want freedom within, it will come with my willingness to allow the child within to heal. Today I know that forgiveness cannot be rushed or imposed and that for me to force it on myself is to do violence to my insides. Part of healing today is to stop making myself act in a way that feels wrong within me.

*I can live with
my feelings as they are.*

It is far better to fight on your feet than on your knees, but you can still fight on your knees.

Aleksandr Solzhenitsyn

Today I will allow myself to enter in. I will not hold back or keep myself on the sidelines. There is no gain for me in affecting a pose of humility that, if the truth were told, is a combination of fear and insecurity. Today my humility will express itself in my willingness to risk, to try and to fail. This is not in just big areas but small ones as well, the smallest interaction in a grocery line, dealing with the little moments in my day, making contact with those around me rather than holding myself in. It is expressing and using my emotions rather than saving them up for who knows what. I can enter the moment in small and big ways.

*I will make a
small move forward.*

Instead of standing on the shore and proving to ourselves that the ocean cannot carry us, let us venture on its waters — just to see.

Pierre Teilhard de Chardin

Truth And Freedom

Today I allow the truth to set me free. I didn't expect enlightenment to hurt like this. I thought that if I became spiritual and free, the pain would not be there. I didn't realize that an important step on my road to freedom was in releasing my beliefs that I own other people, that the world owes me something, that I can control my destiny. I know today what I cannot let go of has a permanent hold on me. I know that no one and nothing really belong to me. Life is a journey and spiritual unfolding is its purpose. I see that my ideas of how things had to be were an illusion and that the time and effort I expended trying to get my life to conform to my illusions kept me from my deeper truth.

I can free myself
from control and illusion.

———

The truth will set you free.
But first it will make you angry.

Anonymous

Having Space In My Relationships

Today I can live with degrees of distance in my close relationships. Intimacy no longer means enmeshment to me. If I am not emotionally sitting on someone else's lap, it doesn't mean I am not getting along with them. That kind of super closeness has a claustrophobic feeling for me now. It worries me because I know that in order to separate and get some breathing room we will have to push hard on one another and it will hurt. I am more comfortable with a little healthy space today. Space used to make me feel abandoned. I felt that if I allowed myself to have some distance, no one would let me in close again. But today I have come to appreciate the freedom it allows me. It is easier to keep those I love in my life when I let go than when I hang on.

I am comfortable with
healthy space.

Those whom we can love, we can hate; to others we are indifferent.

Henry David Thoreau

Letting Go

Today I let go of a problem and trust in a Higher Power. I see that forcing solutions and attempting to control the outcome don't really work to solve anything. Letting go is a spiritual recognition that a power greater than myself is in play. Can I tell the leaves on the trees when to bud or the flowers when to bloom? Am I able to order rain or sunshine and should that power be in my hands? Though I know it is true that I am powerless over nature, I still operate under the illusion that I can control events and the people around me. At best I can arrange my life, but anyone who has lived a little knows that anything can happen.

I can plant a seed and let go of the fruit.

He felt as if he were riding a wave from everything that he knew before, from everything that was familiar.

Elizabeth Winthrop

Today when I get a very strong intuitive message, I will listen to it. I may not be right but I will not discount the feeling or the impulse, knowing that intuition plays an important part in my life. My intuition is real. It is a combination of feelings and instincts that help me to navigate this world. My intuitive sense guides me far more often than I give it credit. Why do I do what I do? Why do I choose certain people over others or plan my life in a particular way? Intuition has a hand in all of this. I will not silence that quiet inner voice with "shoulds" today. Living true to my insides is more comfortable for me than working around them. Intuition is real. It is there to guide me. I will tune in.

I listen to the call inside of me.

———

Lead me from the unreal to the real.
Lead me from darkness to light.
Lead me from death to immortality.
Brihadaranyaka Upanishad

Total Healing

Today I seek more than relief from pain — I seek total healing. While I am only looking to relieve my pain, I will be satisfied when it passes, however it passes, and I will not look for the roots and put in the time and effort necessary for full healing. Total healing comes when I am truly committed to my spiritual growth and deep inner change. Relief from pain is fine, but it is temporary at best; the pain will return in a variety of forms if real healing does not occur. Healing takes patience. It takes a willingness to be completely honest with myself about myself. It means that I have chosen not to run from those parts of me I wish not to see and that I have decided it is more important to be free than relieved.

I seek healing on a deep level.

———

The end of man is to let the spirit in him permeate his whole being, his soul, flesh and affections. He attains his deepest self by losing his selfish ego.

Robert Musil

Today I will remember that when it comes to spirituality the rich get richer and the poor get poorer. When I open my mind and heart to what can be in life, possibilities and good feelings seem to build on each other and increase. When I get caught in negativity, it also increases and I seem to move on a downward cycle. When, on the other hand, situations in my life work out, it appears to follow that other situations work out until it no longer feels like a surprise when things go well. Opening myself to a Higher Power, letting go and trusting produce rewards in my life that increase my own capacity to experience positive change.

I become spiritually richer.

———

The world stands out on either side.
No wider than the heart is wide;
Above the world is stretched the sky
No higher than the soul is high.

Edna St. Vincent Millay

My Own Opinions

Today I understand that I am ultimately my own judge. When I live by the code of others, I become a prisoner of their opinions. Why should I place above my own other people's ideas of who I am and how I should be? Isn't this co-dependency at its very roots — replacing my sense of self with someone else's sense of my self? Perhaps it is a carry-over from childhood when I thought that I was who my parents or society said I was. Today I realize that all of us were mistaken — they, to think that I was supposed to be who they thought I should be, and me, to agree with them and set about acting it out. Other people may have good advice and guidance to share with me but I am the creator within myself.

*I create my being
and my life.*

Who in the world, then, is this man who has any authority to make any declaration about you?

Epictetus

Letting Go Of Worry

Today I recognize the real function that worry serves in my life. When I ruminate over a problem, engage in it, cry, feel pain and lose myself, I feel more alive; I actually experience myself as more in tune and alert when I am upset. I will look for a better path today. Nothing in my life has ever improved through worry, and I have made many situations worse for it. I will make a sincere attempt to intervene on myself when this cycle gets going and let go before I am in its grip.

I can let go of worry.

———

If we did not worry, most of us would feel we were not alive. To be struggling with a problem is for the majority of us an indication of existence. We cannot imagine life without a problem; and the more we are occupied with a problem, the more alert we think we are. . . . Will worry resolve the problem or does the answer . . . come when the mind is quiet?

J. Krishnamurti

Love

Today I release all my concerns, problems and woes to the care of a loving God. There is no need for me to feel constantly burdened if I have faith. Nothing in my life that threatens me will be improved or changed for the better by worry. When I allow a power greater than myself to take over, it is an act of release and surrender that frees my consciousness of turning in on itself. When I do this, I leave some space for air, change, growth and new perceptions.

I can release and turn it over.

I said to the man who stood at the gate of the year: "Give me a light that I may tread safely into the unknown." And he replied, "Go out into the darkness and put your hand into the hand of God. That shall be to you better than a light and safer than a known way."

Minnie L. Haskins
quoted by King George VI
of England on Christmas Day, 1938

I Am Part Of Something Eternal

Today I realize it is my awareness of an eternal truth that opens those doors of knowing to me. While I deny the reality of anything beyond what I can see and touch, that reality is in turn denied to me. If I rest quietly in the joyous awareness that there exists an energy of oneness and unity that can be as close to me as I choose to allow, I can live in eternity right now, recognizing that I am more than the sum of what I see. I always have access to the feeling of connectedness with my Higher Power if I choose to feel that feeling. There is a power greater than me and I am born of that power, ever one with it, ever part of it, ever patterned in its image.

What I am born of I am of.

To the poet, to the philosopher, to the saint, all things are friendly and sacred, all events profitable, all days holy, all men divine.

Ralph Waldo Emerson

Living With Today

Today when I have that nagging feeling that I just cannot fully see and do what is right for me and others, I will see that I probably am right. I simply do not have all the pieces of the puzzle, past, present and future, nor can I have omniscient knowledge of the events and circumstances of my life. How can I always know what is right for me when I don't know for sure what is going to happen? At best I can make an educated guess. Letting go is really the only path I have toward true peace of mind. There simply are no guarantees about anything in life. It is not just a nice idea but a truth and a reality that all I have is the moment. When I try to live beyond the moment, I am mortgaging my present enjoyment and serenity for a wish or a thought of what I hope can be. Is it really worth giving up today for an idea of tomorrow?

I am present for today.

One day at a time.

12-Step slogan

Today I will seek insight and understanding rather than comfort. If all I want is commiseration, I will embed myself deeper in the mire. Instead I will fully accept my pain, whatever it may be, knowing as Buddha taught that it is a condition of life. Running away from it does not take it away. It only forces me to live on the surface of my being. Accepting, even embracing it allows something inside of me to open up. When I allow myself to *experience* a feeling rather than *think about* it, I can move through it. Tension and psychic blocks move aside and insight and the Higher Power have a chance to enter.

I accept the good with the bad.

Life is a test.
It is only a test.
If this were your actual life,
You would have been given better instructions.

Anonymous

I Cannot Identify With Negativity

Today I become aware of the negative forces working though my personality. I am able to see myself in action. When I am being critical, judgmental, jealous or hostile, rather than getting all wrapped up in it, I can take a step back and understand that these thoughts are passing through me but are not of me. Because negativity enters my personality does not mean that I am negative. I need not identify with it. When I do not run from my own negative thoughts, but quietly observe and identify them, I can then let them go. I have not tangled myself with them by engaging in hide-and-seek or tug-of-war. I let them come, look at them and let them go.

*I can release myself from
the grip of negativity.*

The one thing evil cannot stand is for you to quietly observe it in yourself, without self-condemnation, without panic and without fight.
                                    Vernon Howard

Letting Go Of Preconceptions

Today I will live life without a script. I will sink back into the moment and let it be. I will allow my own spontaneity to emerge and enable me to participate in situations in ways that are appropriate and allow for my own aliveness. When I do not presuppose each event that I walk into, life becomes endlessly new. I have let myself become hypnotized by ideas of who I should be, what life should be and what those around me should be. This kind of habitual thinking does not allow me to see life as more than the sum of my thoughts about life. Today I am willing to enter experience in a new way — I let go of my preconceived ideas and see life through childlike eyes.

I see life in a new way.

The courage not to believe in anything.
Ivan Sergeyevich Turgenev

No More Fog

Today I no longer keep myself in a fog to protect myself from my own painful and anxious feelings. Part of my fog was expressed in an inability to get little things done, in being late, in having trouble making decisions, then second guessing them. Other aspects of my fog were not having clear answers to questions or not really knowing what I was feeling. I found it hard to be straight with other people and ask for what I wanted. Since I have been willing to feel my buried feelings in recovery, the fog has cleared. It was hard to go through the feelings but worth it to have myself back on a day-to-day basis.

I enjoy being with myself.

If a man harbors any sort of fear, it makes him landlord to a ghost.

Lloyd Douglas

Today I make a small positive effort. If the efforts that I make are not coming from a good place inside of me, they will get me nowhere. If I make negative efforts born out of attitudes that are not helpful, no matter how hard I work at them, it will yield little positive change in my life. Much less effort in the right direction will yield quicker and better results. If I calm and clear my mind so that, by slowing it down, I can actually see what is in it, I will get a feeling for what needs to be done and what direction would be most fruitful for me to take.

I make less but better effort.

———

Human nature is not a machine to be built after a model and set to do exactly the work prescribed for it, but a tree, which requires to grow and develop itself on all sides, according to the tendency of the inward forces which make it a living thing.

John Stuart Mill

Protecting Myself

Today I have different ways of listening and responding to protect myself from over-exposure to other people's pain and stress. There is a way of being empathetic without losing myself. If I truly allow myself to let go as I listen, to know that someone else has their own Higher Power and it's not me, I can turn the person I am trying to respond to over in my mind and heart. Much as I would like, I cannot be everything to everyone and I am unable to be more than one place at a time. In my co-dependency I felt that to help someone else I had to take on their problems and make them my own. Today I see that that does not help them or me; in fact, it creates a third sort of problem — that of unentangling the mess of my feelings layered on top of and around the sides of theirs.

I can change the way
I listen and assist.

———

True eloquence consists in saying
all that should be said, and that only.
La Rochefoucauld

Today I understand that I was not able to claim my autonomy as a child in healthy ways. When I tried to put needed and healthy distance in my relationships with my parents, it bothered them, I suppose, because it made them feel rejected, activating their own abandonment issues, and because they thought I would never come back. Rather than support me in my journey away from them and toward myself, they rejected me for pushing them away. It made it so frightening for me to separate that I devised ways of only sort of separating. I reasoned out in my childlike mind that separation meant rejection and that I would lose the relationships I loved completely if I allowed myself to feel separate. I thought that to be close to someone I had to be like them.

I can allow myself to feel separate.

———

Every real object must cease to be what it seemed and none could ever be what the whole soul desired.

George Santayana

My Own Physician

Today I recognize that I am my own best physician. Within me lives an internal healer that knows all it needs to about my inner workings, my psychological blocks and inner trauma. When I am ready to look at myself, that data will be revealed to me. I have ways to release pain built into me. I can cry, mourn, feel ill, release anger and fully allow my being to express the stored pain, rage and grief that are in my way. When I do this, I will again be in possession of the good and strong sides of myself and memories that I had been unable to feel. I do not need to be afraid of what is inside of me . . . it is only more of me.

I can look at my own insides.

———

One must raise the self by the self.
And not let the self sink down.
For the self's only friend is the self
And the self is the self's one enemy.

Bhagavadgita

Today I refuse to beat myself up because I have in some way made an error. I needn't fall apart on the inside. When I go on and on berating myself, one mistake becomes ten, and soon I have burrowed myself in so deep that I can't get out. This time when I do something that I find upsetting, I will let the torment end there. Being thrown off once by a thing gone wrong is enough; repeating it over and over again is compulsive and self-destructive. There is just no reason to be so hard on myself — who will benefit from it? My refusal to allow myself to fall into an inward cycle of negativity over an outward error makes a healthy, self-affirming statement that I am ready to live in harmony with myself and keep my life on a positive track.

I am not hard on my own insides.

———

The greatest part of our happiness or misery depends on our dispositions and not on our circumstances.

Martha Washington

Trusting My Gut Feelings

Today I know that I am not crazy if the message that I feel is denied by those sending it. Sometimes people act out feelings that they lack either the courage or the awareness to put into words. Consequently, I get one strong message on the gut level and a completely different one in action. This can make me feel crazy when I mistrust my insides and believe what I am told. Recovery has taught me to trust my intuitive feelings, not to silence them and force a kind of reason on myself that doesn't make any sense to my insides. Today I can accept that there might be two stories, the one being told and the one being acted out. I do not need to try to get my feelings to go along with someone else's, nor do I need their approval and agreement to have my own truth. I can quietly entertain my sense of things without convincing everyone else to see things my way.

I let myself have my feelings.

———

Trust in God but tie your camel.

Persian proverb

Today I will remember that when I encounter someone who is overheated with angry feeling, I can stay clear and calm and it will not pass to me. Because someone else is having a hard day need not mean that I have to have one too. If I am not a willing receptacle for another person's angry feelings, they can pass me by. If they connect with my own angry feelings that I deny by using their anger to mask my own, I will prolong the agony for both of us. Then I need to understand where my anger is coming from and own it. If the anger truly is not mine, I can protect myself by not heating up to its level. I don't need to get defensive to fend it off — I can fend it off by not becoming it.

*I can live with
another person's anger.*

———

*Heat cannot of itself pass
from a colder to a hotter body.*
Rudolph Julius Emanuel Clasius

My Own Decisions

Today I will make my decisions about how I want to lead my day. Having an agenda of my own that pleases me is a good thing. If I am rigid and inflexible and ask others to follow my agenda whether or not it suits them, I am training them to be co-dependent, and I am being compulsive and dependent on plans. If I cannot allow myself to plan my own day and wait to fit myself into everyone else's day, I am co-dependent. Today I will know what I would like my day to look like and understand that there will be other factors to consider. Without my own plan, I will lose a sense of "self." Without flexibility, I will lose a sense of "other." To be happy, I need to be in comfortable rapport with both my inner self and my sense of other in my life.

I look at how I live my day.

———

The art of pleasing is the art of deceiving.
Vauvenargues

Higher Source Of Wisdom

*T*oday when life gets rough, I will remind myself that I am not in it alone — someone besides me understands and sees and I can turn to that power within me at any moment to lighten my own burden. I learn in program to begin each day by turning my troubles over to a higher source. This is what I will do today. Before I act out of fear and anxiety and deepen whatever problems I am in the midst of, I will release them into the loving and wiser hands of a universal wisdom. Even if I don't believe and trust that anything can improve, the mere act of turning over will lift me up.

I look to a higher
source for help.

———

Experience is the worst teacher; it gives the test before presenting the lesson.

Vernon Law

Deep Fears

Today I accept that life is a painful teacher. Perhaps more than anything else, I see my deepest fears manifest in my life. It is almost as if I create those situations continually until I learn to take the charge out of them for myself. The painful part of the experiment is to know which part of what I see is real and which is a manifestation of my fears and is therefore partially illusionary. When my fears come out in life, they look bigger and scarier than ever. Though they are frightening enough in my dreams, when they manifest in my day-to-day reality, I feel them and that can be terrifying. I understand today that I can survive my feelings — they are not all of me.

*I will dispel
my deepest fears with
love and acceptance.*

A proverb is a short sentence based on long experience.

Miguel de Cervantes

Today I realize that negativity has a psychic life of its own. When I focus on it and think about it, I am nurturing and allowing it to grow strong and formidable in my life. Negativity is real and it feeds on strength and goodness. Today I am stronger than that which is not of God. I align myself with the wisdom, power and beauty of a Higher Force, and I truly believe that light and love can make a friend of darkness. Where there are problems in my life, I will rise to my full strength. I move into my own heart, center myself in prayer and align myself with a loving universe.

**I am stronger
in love than negativity.**

---

*A little neglect may breed great mischief —
For want of a nail, the shoe was lost;
And for want of a horse, the rider was lost.*

Benjamin Franklin

Growing Through

Today I let light into my life. I understand that the attitudes and thoughts that I take to my day are formative in creating my experience. I will dare to think positively today. As a child with a painful past, life working out is more frightening to me than having problems. That early trauma of having my family go through pain lives inside of me like a deep well of sorrow. I will pray for healing in this place within me, letting the pain go, turning it over to a higher source. I will grow through the experience and know that it has taught me deep and beautiful lessons. Then I will make room for good.

I can grow through
life experience.

———

It is the highest creatures who take the longest to mature, and are the most helpless during their immaturity.

George Bernard Shaw

Today I will not avoid an inner hell in order to live constantly in heaven. When I refuse my deepest fears and nightmares, I keep the best of my inner life at bay as well. The demons that I fear the most gain life while I hold them in the darkness within me. When I face them fully and bring them into the light they shrivel up and die. Part of my psychic and spiritual growth lies in my willingness to know all — all that is outside and all that is within. Running from any part of me creates distance from my soul — if I wish to walk a spiritual path and come closer to myself, I need to face all that is there. There is nothing ugly about me if I hold it in the light of compassion, love and forgiveness; no hell on earth or within me is more powerful ultimately than love.

I will face fully
what is inside of me.

———

Hell has three gates: lust, anger and greed.
Bhagavadgita

Self-Respect

Today I realize that self-respect is pivotal to a healthy and happy personality. When I have self-respect, I have the ability to say no. When I have boundaries and can say no, then and only then can I really say yes. When I can say yes, the world opens up to me. I can be humble when I have self-respect. I can do what is appropriate and needed in a situation because I am not tied up in impressing other people or proving anything to them. When I have self-respect, I silently let others know how I expect to be treated. When I am with someone who cares about themselves, we both feel more comfortable. Other people tend to see me as I see myself. Today I feel I am entitled to my self-respect.

I feel good about myself.

Be a friend to thyself, and others will be so too.

Thomas Fuller

Today I will ask for a miracle. I trust that nothing is more real in this universe than the love and the power of God. I understand that the medium of miracles and shifts in perception is prayer. I will clear my mind of all negativity and ask for what I really need. In the past I have not dared to ask for enough but today is different. With love in my heart, I bring my problem into focus. I look at it, and I ask for a true shift in perception. I wish no one harm, including myself. Still I need help, help to see what I am not seeing, help to release the cloud of doubt and negativity that surrounds me on this issue, help to set my mind free of fear and anxiety.

I pray for a miracle.

———

The direction of the mind is more important than its progress.

Joseph Joubert

Rewriting The Past

Today I will rewrite a traumatic past event to neutralize it in my mind. My unconscious does not know the difference between what really happened and what I reprogram into it. I recreate patterns in my present that are unconscious patterns held from my past. Part of working out past issues is bringing them to a conscious level and feeling the old pain. The next step is to let it go so that the pattern is neutralized and released. I can reconstruct an event by playing it through my mind the way I wish it had been. Recovery is more than understanding the past — it is also about actually revisualizing and reprogramming the past. When I replace a positive inner experience for a negative one, I am telling the universal forces that this is who I am.

I can reprogram my unconscious.

Nothing changes more consistently than the past. The past that influences our lives is not what actually happened but what we believe happened.

Gerald W. Johnson

Changing Painful Dynamics

Today I recognize the futility of trying to change someone else's behavior. If I postpone my own growth and happiness until such time when others close to me recognize what I am doing, approve of it and act as I wish they would, I might wait forever. If someone else *could* act better, they *would* act better. What they are doing is all they can do. If they are behaving in unenlightened ways, it is because they are not able to do otherwise. They lack self-awareness. Their awareness will come to them in their own time. What I can do is change my behavior. If there is a dynamic that I do not like, I will do far more to alter it by clearing up my side. When I don't engage in my part of a difficult interaction, it transforms into something else.

I will change myself.

———

Growth is the only evidence of life.
John Henry Newman

283

A Change In Perception

Today I recognize that it is not simply the contents of my life that determine my inner peace and happiness, but how I see those contents. Often a shift in perception is worth more than changing my circumstance. When I see what is outside of me as determining my happiness, I enter into a control battle with the people, places and things that fill my life. Moving these around will not necessarily make me more comfortable. First I will examine the way that I am seeing things. Do I need to change my circumstance or the way that I am seeing my circumstance?

*I am willing
to experience a change
in perception.*

The fool sees not the same tree a wise man sees.

William Blake

Being One With God

Today I see that truth and love are constant and more powerful than illusion. It is my belief in the illusion that keeps me powerless. I am a child of God in the most real sense. This is a status that I share with my parents, my grandparents, my children — even plants and animals. There is a benevolent force that has given birth to us all, and we are one with it. God is a force that lives within me and in my heart I have always known that. It is for me today to recognize fully my nature as of God as well as other living creatures.

I am one with God.

———

In my father's house there
are many mansions. I go to prepare
a place for you. And you yourself know
the way where I am going.

John 14:2

Trust In Higher Sources

Today I let life flow through me. I am not the generator but the transmitter of energy. There are sources beyond my imagination that I can draw from — all I need do is to open myself. I am not alone, and life is not confined only to what I see. When I open my inner vision and ask forces that I cannot see but that I can sense to guide, sustain and protect me, I experience serenity and a sense of well-being. I am energized by the understanding that I am not alone and that I can call for help and support from spiritual sources. While I cannot necessarily see them, I trust that they are there.

I trust in what
I cannot see.

———

The only real faith is blind faith.

Anonymous

Tolerating The Anxiety Of Change

Today I accept that life is full of transitions. As a child, change came to mean trauma. I never knew what to expect in my dysfunctional home. Would all be calm and loving or would everyone be frantic, tense and at each other's throats? Either was possible. Both were unpredictable and frightening — the good, because if I let myself feel the wonderful love, peace and calm, I immediately feared the terrible pain of losing it. The bad, because we tore at one another with our arguing, rage and insults. At some deep level I put my trust in the bad; it hurt too much to trust the good and lose it over and over again. Today when I get scared over a transition, I see that it's about old pain. I needn't get stuck in it again. I have tools today that I didn't have then.

I can tolerate the anxiety that change brings up.

—

Genius is formed in quiet, character in the stream of life.

Johann Wolfgang von Goethe

Thought Power

Today I fully recognize the immense power of thought. That which I dwell upon I become. My thoughts have more power to impact and create my reality than I realize. Doing is just the extension of thinking. I will first create in my mind what I would like to see in my life for both myself and those I love. My thoughts are creative energy, and when I take responsibility for them, I take responsibility for my life. The inner beliefs about myself and others that I hold in my mind will eventually find their way into my day-to-day reality. I will have the courage today to be aware of and take responsibility for the contents of my mind. I will take ownership of who I am.

I believe in the
creative power of thought.

The secret thoughts of a man run over all things, holy, profane, clean, obscure, grave and light, without shame or blame.

Thomas Hobbes

Today I recognize that spirituality is not so much a question of doing as of being. It is not where I am going to as much as where I am coming from that counts. God-centered living is a space that I live in, in my mind. There is nothing to prove by doing. There is no circumstance to manipulate that can show that I am close to or far from Higher Power. Living in the presence of light, love and compassion is what it is all about. I can take a thousand actions that look right, but if the heart that directs my hand is coming from an empty place, then all of those actions have less spiritual impact than just one that comes from a spiritual and loving place.

I am being where
I want to be.

___

The things we know best are those we have not learned.

Vauvenargues

Knowing Myself

Today I love myself for having reached this distance. Life is not easy, none of us escapes pain. In my understanding of this and my willingness to embrace and live with pain, I have not missed the joy, the beauty, the poetry of the moment. Life for me has been a rich experience because I have not asked it to be what it is not. I am proud that I have wrangled with life, that I have not tried to make it all fit into a neat and antiseptic little package that looks good but is dry to the taste. For today I am not afraid because I am not hiding from myself. I have not avoided my worst depths — what more is there to frighten me? I take comfort in the knowledge that I have looked as far as I can see. I am not a stranger to myself.

I let myself know who I am.

Out-worn heart, in a time out-worn,
Come clear of the nets of wrong and right;
Laugh, heart, again in the grey twilight;
Sigh, heart, again in the dew of morn.

W. B. Yeats

Today I am aware that it is more difficult to let go of a painful, dysfunctional situation or relationship than a happy, healthy one. When a relationship or situation is going wrong, I become entangled in the mess, always feeling that if I did just a little bit more, if I tried a little harder, if I changed something . . . then it would work. When I come from this insecure place, it really never does work out . . . all of my frantic efforts only serve to complicate an already complicated situation and my best intentions fall on deaf ears. Letting go does not mean losing; it simply means that I am willing for change to occur. Sometimes the change is so subtle I only know it took place because I feel better; sometimes it is more pronounced.

I can let go and
allow movement to occur.

———

If error is corrected whenever it is recognized as such, the path of error is the path of truth.

Hans Reichenbach

Releasing Myself

Today I understand that it is only when I can let something be that it can let me be. So much of my life happens in my own mind, though I live with the illusion that everything happens outside of me. When I truly observe that outer change has its first origins within my mind, I begin to see how the whole thing really works. It is when I am able to make a deep, personal decision and accept it with my whole being — willing to allow that decision to find its way into my life — that invisible forces go to work to bring it into being. What I believe to be true about myself and my life in the privacy of my own mind has a profound effect on my life on the outside. What I can let go of can let go of me.

I let whatever binds me go.

Life was never meant to be a struggle; just a gentle progression from one point to another, much like walking through a valley on a sunny day.

Stuart Wilde

Today I do not need to have everything I love in my life at every moment. Because I care about something, a relationship, a house, a situation, does not mean that I am going to lose it. I trust now that people, places and things in life come and go. That is the nature of it all. Nothing I can do will change that. When I learn to roll with the natural vicissitudes of life, they somehow feel less threatening. I am more willing to allow people, places and things be removed from me because I have come to understand that they will return in the same or different forms. Today I know that that is true; it is the nature of life. But it is a loss that is constantly filled with gain.

I let go so that
I can be filled again.

———

Nothing in the world lasts save eternal change.
Honorat de Bueil, Marquis de Racan

How Important Is It?

Today I will remember to ask myself, "How important is it?" before I let myself get upset or angry about something. When I allow my feelings to run ahead of my senses and forget that I need to keep them in balance, I run the risk of producing the very circumstances that I fear in my life. Is it really worth what it will cost me and those around me to enlarge on a problem that might arise? There are so many things that I feel almost honor bound to get upset about — as if in not getting upset I am betraying myself. Today I realize that nothing is worth giving up my serenity — that is the most important thing for me not to lose.

I put my serenity
ahead of getting even.

———

The cheerful loser is the winner.

George Herbert

Today I will open myself to receive. Much of what I experience as lack in my life is really my inability to see life as constantly giving to me. When I put myself into a receptive state, what blocks do I place in my own path? Do I feel worthy of a healthy, happy life? Do I trust that it is possible for life to work out? Am I able to visualize a good life? Am I willing to forego my attachment to negativity and control so that my life can be fully positive? Really this universe is already abundant. Nature is constantly striving to produce — to meet my needs. My ability to open myself to receive this generosity and abundance is how I clear the channels for it to come to me. My ability to recognize it and to be grateful for it is how I hold it in my life.

*I open myself to receive
all good that is coming to me.*

———

The empires of the future are the empires of the mind.

Winston Churchill

Being With My Feelings

Today I will allow whatever is flowing through me to flow. I will move aside my agenda of who I think I should be and be where I am. I will create an atmosphere within me of self-acceptance, not attempting to line myself up in any particular direction but observing how I do line up. I do not need to control myself on the inside today. When I watch rather than tangle with my thoughts, I lessen my reactivity. I might spend hours, even days resisting, thinking or feeling a certain way while, if I just accepted whatever it is I am resisting and allowed myself to feel it fully, it would probably pass through me in a matter of minutes and I would be free of it.

*I will process and be with
what is already there.*

Tell us your phobias and we will tell you what you are afraid of.

Robert Benchley

Losing My Life To Find It

Today I see that in spiritual growth I lose my life to find it. This is just the opposite of establishing my identity in a worldly way, which lies in surrounding myself with things that I want to represent me. In this way I define and seek a sense of self through representation. I know now that I cannot find me in a reflection of myself. When I do this, my eyes are constantly focused outward, and I forget that it is through an inner gazing that I come to know who I am and what life is all about. The sense of loss I may experience when I cease looking for my true identity in objects outside myself disappears when I look within for my life and meaning.

*I let go of my
smaller self to know
my larger self.*

In my end is my beginning.

T. S. Eliot

Accepting Abundance

Today I will accept abundance in my life. The more that I recognize abundance as being meant for me, the more it will be for me. An unconscious attitude of limitation and scarcity will find its way into my life if I allow it to. When I can see the prosperity in this world as a boundless supply, one in which I partake along with others, I open the channels for it to enter into my life. I will think positively about other people's prosperity, knowing that what I believe to be true for someone else, I also believe to be true for me. In fact, any thought that I think about another person I first create and accept within my own mind as a possibility and a truth.

I accept the
abundance in my life.

———

The moon belongs to everyone,
The best things in life are free.

B. G. DeSylva

Knowing Myself

Today I accept myself as I am. When I live by a self-flattering set of images and deny my own negative qualities, I never truly know myself. Consequently I never truly know others. To only know what is flattering about myself keeps me forever on the surface of life and in bondage to my own unwillingness to see. Accepting what is the worst in me tends to transform it in some way because I no longer feed it by keeping it in darkness. When I expose it to light, it changes. When I will only know a self-aggrandizing side of myself, that is all I can know in others. When I am able to live with all of it — to know myself fully — then I develop wisdom and acceptance and I can see who another person is.

I will live with all of me.

---

anyone lived in pretty how town
(with up so floating many bells down)
spring summer autumn winter
he sang his didn't he danced his did

e. e. cummings

Gratitude

Today I will begin my day consciously. When I wake up, I will not just roll out of bed and into my morning. Each day I am alive is a gift and I choose to recognize it as such. I love my life. I have so much to be thankful for. Rather than swim around in emptiness, I will sit in the presence of plenty. When I appreciate what I have, I support and create it in my life. The universe loves a good receiver and a generous heart. What I am truly appreciative of in my life has a way of continuing to come to me.

I am grateful and make it known.

———

Now when I awaken and before I even open my eyes, I thank the bed for a good night's sleep. Then with my eyes still closed, I spend about ten minutes just being thankful for all the good in my life. I program my day a bit, affirming that everything will go well and that I will enjoy it all. This is before I get up and do my morning meditation or prayers.

Louise Hay

Today I accept my true nature as a free person — free to create my own life not based on the expectations of others, ideas in books or images in the media. I am here to explore the mysteries of the universe that are contained within my own being. When I take a spiritual path and study who I am and my own divine nature, I am exploring the universe. It takes more courage for me to go inward than to traverse the world because my interior reality is the most profoundly unknown to me. Diving into my own unconscious is no less scary than diving into the depths of the sea. This is a terrible and frightening journey, the journey inward, but it is filled with more beauty than I have ever known. At the other end of the night sweats, the labyrinth, the terror, is space, peace and a divine sort of nothing.

I take my own freedom.

———

I am tired of ruling over slaves.

Last words of
Frederick the Great

Sacred Awe

Today I see that the goal of life is spiritual unity with all things. It is to know that I am an inextricable part of God and that God, or a central energy or one organizing power, is all that there is. Everything that I take in through my senses has as its source this singular energy. God is an energy, ever changing, ever masquerading as variety, ever present in all things. The feeling of love, peace, unity or oneness approaches the experience of God. The experience of these feelings — the sitting, knowing and being in the presence of God — is just that. It is tuning into that energy which has the power to nurture, hold and love me as nothing else can.

I can see and be with
this magnificent world.

———

The highest point a man can attain is not knowledge or virtue or goodness or victory, but something even greater, more heroic and more despairing: Sacred Awe!

Nikos Kazantzakis

Today I accept and understand that life is both pain and joy. Sometimes recovery creates the impression that one day I should be free of pain, and I feel "unrecovered" when I still have problems in my life. The goal is not to be free from pain, which is a given in life, but to live with pain differently. In recovery the real lesson is not how to avoid problems but how to work them through and let them go more quickly. Problems are a part of life, but are not all of life. There is as much happiness and beauty in life as ugliness. Recovery is about not avoiding either — it's about eliminating old debris so I can experience life in the present and gain wisdom from a painful past.

**_I accept life
on its own terms._**

_Man was made for joy and woe,
And when this we rightly know
Through the world we safely go._

William Blake

I Learn To Know

Today I make myself my greatest mentor. It is the decisions that I make in the quiet of my own mind that most profoundly affect my day-to-day life. I will not be guided by a thousand outside voices today. Though I am open to counsel and advice, I guide my own life. When I place more weight and faith in other people's sense of who I am and how I should live than in my own, I rob myself of my greatest treasure, my own common sense. I know better than anyone what I am capable of doing, feeling and carrying out. When I keep my own strength and conviction within me, when I do not give it away, I am someone to reckon with. I have solidity.

I learn from experience
and know from tuning in.

Never believe on faith, see for yourself!
What you yourself don't learn, you don't know.

Bertolt Brecht

Today I know that what I accumulate in my life is of no account if I lose my spirit, my self, my soul. I can enjoy the things of the world when I see them for what they are and do not ask them to be more than they are or to give me what they cannot give. They are meant to enhance my pleasure, not to be the source of it. It is my knowledge and awareness of that part of me which is infinite that is my true source of peace, pleasure, happiness and serenity. When I am in full possession of this inner self, which is also connected to the universal self, then I am in a position to take pleasure in the world around me.

I am that which never dies.

We brought nothing into this world. And it is certain we carry nothing out of it.

1 Timothy 6:7

The Here And Now

*T*oday I see that all of life, love, wisdom and God are contained in each moment. There is nowhere to go, nothing to do and no one to be. All that I require to be a saint or sage is alive in the here and now. In fact, the here and now is the only place that is alive. It is my access to all that is infinite and all that is life. When I look for life in the past or the future, it is simply not there because all things remain in the moment, the point where my own being intersects with the forces of all life. I experience it through my senses, and I know it through my soul.

I see all in the here and now.

To see a world in a grain of sand
And a heaven in a wild flower,
Hold infinity in the palm of your hand
And eternity in an hour.

William Blake

What Lies Next To My Hand

Today I will do what is in front of me. Rather than make my plan for the day on a formless future, I will do that task which is nearest to my hand. I cannot live in days that have not happened yet. Hard as I try, I cannot put my boots on and take a walk through the future. Life unfolds as it is meant to, and the life that I lead is subject to the laws of time. Time is actually a wonderful caring principle that gives me my life in manageable doses. To understand and experience the depth of the moment — to taste the sweet that is in my hand — that is living. The rest will be provided for.

I perform the task in front of me.

Do the Duty which lies nearest thee,
Which thou knowest to be a Duty!
Thy Second Duty will already
*   have become clearer . . .*

Thomas Carlyle

Drinking In Life

Today I will drink. I will drink of the wisdom alive in the day, in the tiny moments of pure beauty that I experience when I am still, the comfort and love available in the eyes of friends. I will not ask that happiness remain but will take pleasure in its fleeting nature; when it comes, I will enjoy it fully, and when it disappears, I will let it go, knowing that it will return. This world is meant for me to enjoy. When I was a child, I deeply understood this, but as I grew into an adult, I came to feel that the riches of life were kept in a box — perhaps available to others, perhaps available to me at some later date or maybe just to look at the box and wonder.

*I will not walk by
happiness and beauty.*

———

I am dying of thirst by the side of the fountain.

Charles d'Orleans

Today I place my heart, life and soul in the care of a loving God, a benevolent universe that has my good at heart. When I entrust my happiness to situations, allowing their vicissitudes to tell me whether or not I feel good about myself, or sell my soul for an idea or a thing, I "gain the world but lose my soul." I become a beggar within my own being, waiting for other people to hand me a portion of myself. Today I am aware that the treasures of serenity, wisdom, strength and goodness that lie within me will outlast anything I collect on the outside.

I am alive to my own inner beauty.

———

Lay not up for yourselves treasures upon earth, where moth and rust doth corrupt, and where thieves break through and steal: But lay up for yourselves treasures in heaven . . . For where your treasure is, there will your heart be also.

Matthew 6:19–21

Becoming Aware

Today I will become aware of the extent to which I am a prisoner of my own thoughts. Thoughts are a creation of the mind, and when I think I am only the sum total of my thoughts, then life comes to feel habitual and dull. There is a pure energy that belongs to stillness and that moves in when I observe rather than actively engage in my thinking process. When my mind is still, I feel a meditative, psychic flow that seems to come from nowhere. Though the person that I am comes from my own unique combination of thoughts, I can tune into a central intelligence energy that is beyond me. This is my own personal Higher Power. Not an autocratic, disembodied entity, but a benevolent, ever-present force that is there whenever I can be available to it.

I can tune in.

———

A life of faith . . . enables us to see God in everything and it holds the mind in a state of readiness for whatever may be His will.
François Fenelon

Today I slow down my mental processes so that I can become aware of the contents of my mind. While my mind is racing, it is lost to me, out of my control. I endlessly chase it in an effort to somehow bring it back. I understand now that chasing it only gets me further lost. When I feel restless and anxious, I will take it as a signal that I need some quiet, still time. I will sit down, center myself and wait for the mental chatter and noise to subside. I will not attempt to control or engage in my overdrive mental activity. I allow it to pass by my inner field of vision like a flowing river, apart from me, on its own way. I will even out my breathing and be aware of how my serenity restores itself. I do not need to do more.

I return to
peacefulness within.

We do without doing and everything gets done.

Donald Blume

Craving

Today I recognize that constantly craving things keeps me locked in a cycle of binging and purging the stuff of life. The world can only give me so much. My true happiness lies in the realization and communion with my self and my Higher Power. When I think that I need a new car, house or person in order to be happy, I am not recognizing that my real happiness does not depend upon moving the externals of my life around. When I am at peace with myself, I will be able to see clearly what I need to create for satisfaction. I will let go of the feeling that I will only be happy when I give all my power away to things and people outside myself. Contentment is an inside job; until I can feel it within me, nothing I do outside will have a lasting effect.

*I see craving
as a cycle of self-abuse.*

———

What poison is to food, self-pity is to life.
Oliver C. Wilson

Today I understand that I cannot tie everything into a neat and tidy package, nor should that be my goal. *Vive la différence* can mean all sorts of differences. What is interesting about my life is its endless variety. There is such a rich banquet in front of me, why do I want so badly to order it and bring it down to a smaller size? When I allow what is just to be and trust that there is plenty there to taste as I go along — that I needn't eat it all today nor somehow avoid its richness — I get so much more out of life. Life is not meant to be gulped and lived and understood all in the same afternoon, but to be tasted and savored a little at a time.

> *I move through*
> *my life day by day.*

> *How can you govern*
> *a country which has 246*
> *varieties of cheese?*

Charles de Gaulle

The Pulsating Force Of Life

Today I will not second-guess each word that comes out of my mouth and each action that passes through my hand. When I over-analyze my life, it loses something. Life is meant to be experienced first and understood later. When I pay more attention to how I think about my life than how it feels from moment to moment, the actual life force flows through me without my being in touch with it. I become locked in my mind running from thought to thought in a crazy search for meaning. When I have a full body experience of life, what goes through my head about it is secondary. I am alive and that is enough.

I am in touch with
life within me.

———

Let's not get into paralysis through analysis. Let's leave some space for God to walk through the room.

· Quincy Jones

Today I will take time to smell the roses. Why should I wait until I am close to death to understand what is valuable in life? Why should I postpone seeing life for what it is? Life is really what happens between the cracks. It is the quiet moments of real perception, of seeing what is there all the time but passed over. It is that unexplainable feeling deep in the heart that pulls on the soul and makes me feel alive and in touch. These moments do not come from my running around and searching them out — they come when I am still, tuned in and waiting. They come when I invite them into my day.

*I will leave room
for magic.*

———

*What is this life if, full of care,
We have no time to stand and stare.*

W. H. Davies

A Scientific Approach To Life

Today I understand that I live by trial and error. I will act like a scientist in my own life, conducting little and big experiments to see what does and doesn't work. If I am able to learn from mistakes, then they need not be the end of the story. It is difficult when I see that something works, to get myself to believe in it and try it again. What doesn't work can sometimes feel more familiar and even more comfortable to me than what does, and often I find myself repeating that pattern rather than a more constructive one. Though I do not fully understand my tendency to do this, for today I will assume that habit is very powerful. Changing habits will involve effort.

*I am able to work
to change habits.*

———

Now there is one outstandingly important fact regarding Spaceship Earth, and that is that no instruction book came with it.

Buckminster Fuller

316

Worry And Fretting

Today, as a favor to myself, I am not going to worry. When I let myself get stressed out over situations or things that other people do — though I may make them back off, feel unhappy or become concerned about me — is it really worth it? There is no getting even. When I fret and cogitate, the person I really get even with is me. If I set myself up in opposition to other people, I may get some satisfaction at having got their attention, but it does not really fulfill my deeper need to feel centered and secure. I may feel engaged and connected with them, which makes me feel less lonely, but to accomplish this I have lost myself and the easygoing relationship with them that I have had under better circumstances.

I don't sweat the little ones.

———

Be not angry that you cannot make others as you wish them to be, since you cannot make yourself as you wish you to be.

Thomas à Kempis

317

Dreams And Fantasies

Today I am able to let go of the fantasy of what "could be" in my intimate relationships. Having had the stages of successful parent-child relationships interrupted — not learning that we can be different, separate people and still love one another — I enter my intimate relationships with the hope and expectation that they can give me what I didn't get; that a relationship will not disappoint me. Unfortunately, in not actually having had successful relationships as a child, I don't know what is normal to expect as an adult. I lack an easy sense of give and take — a basic understanding of what should or should not be tolerated. Unfortunately, because I'm not sure what to look for, I am also not sure when I have found it. I will give the relationships I have a chance.

I examine my life with an observant eye.

The great law of culture is: Let each become all that he was created capable of being.
Thomas Carlyle

318

Today I will allow myself to change my old chaotic behaviors. If there had been a motto in my family of origin, it might have read something like "keep the chaos." I find that I currently live this motto out in my life. Whenever my life threatens to be too peaceful or things are a bit too smooth, a little voice in the back of my head instructs me to mess it up. I am able to see today that this is a repetition of a way of living in my family that belongs to my past and need not belong to my present. I will allow myself to see the many little ways that I keep chaos alive in my life, then I will change my behavior.

I let go of
old repeated chaos.

———

Living well is the best revenge.

George Herbert

My Internal Spectator

Today I will become one with my own internal spectator — that part of me which observes the working of my own mind and thoughts. There is a part of me that watches the way I operate. When I, in a way, become that observing role, I gain a sense of relief and distance from the burden of my own thoughts. It is refreshing to enter into the part of my mind that does not identify with each passing thought, but simply watches it as it goes by without trying to act, judge or control. I learn about myself through my own dispassionate self-observation. I find it less threatening to change my behavior when I don't feel so overly identified with it.

I am more than
my thoughts and behavior.

———

Plato, Aristotle and Socrates are Secretaries of Nature.

James Howell

Today I will do things that please me. When I think about "getting a life together," it seems like an overwhelming tall order — really more that I can conceive of or do. What is "a life" anyway? I feel much more able to act on my own behalf if I take it one day at a time. What I decide to do in a day that I care about and want to do is, after all, a life — my life. If I think of getting a life as only a huge long-term goal, I will miss doing all the little things along the way that make me feel that I actually do have a life. There are a variety of ways to get a life: long-term goals, short-term goals and today's activities.

*I see that having a life
is having it now.*

———

Live all you can; it's a mistake not to. It doesn't so much matter what you do in particular, so long as you have your life. If you haven't had that, what have you had?

Henry James

Self-Neglect

Today I see that when I want to give up and throw away everything I have worked for, I am acting out of self-neglect. When I put myself aside in service of a situation, I don't really serve it. Negating myself is not healthy for myself or anyone else. When I discount myself and want everyone else, I throw a situation out of balance. Rather than living out of my desires, I brush myself aside and look at everyone else's day as more important than my own. I allow their wants and needs to overwhelm my own, and in so doing I neglect to meet mine and I resent them when they meet theirs.

*I will pay
attention to myself.*

Anywhere is the center of the earth.

Black Elk

Today I will intervene on my various forms of self-abuse both subtle and gross. When I do to myself what I resent others having done to me, I am doing self-harm. When I am too hard on myself for a mistake; when I ruminate over problems without putting them aside after a while; when I deny myself the right to feel good about something I have done; when I constantly tell myself that I am not good enough; when I do not get the rest and quiet I need because I have too much to do and think I am the only one who can or will do it — I am abusing myself. I begin by treating myself this way, then I inevitably treat others the same way.

*I recognize my forms
of self-abuse.*

How many ideas go unexplored because people lack the courage to fail?

Wilbur M. McFeely

Subtle Shifts

Today I will search for a Higher Power in the subtle moments and quiet spaces. I will remember that God works in mysterious ways, and I will look for those situations and coincidences that are not accidental but really reflect a spirit at work. When I open myself to what I really need and become willing to allow God into my life, there are so many ways that He begins to materialize. I will pay attention today to this process at work in my life.

*I see the hand of
my Higher Power at work.*

---

*We apprehend Him in the alternate voids
and fullness of a cathedral; in the space that
separates the salient features of a picture; in
the living geometry of a flower, a sea shell,
an animal; in the pauses and intervals between the notes of music, on the plane of
conduct, in the love and gentleness, the confidence and humility, which give beauty to the
relationships between human beings.*

Aldous Huxley

Today I remind myself of the deep relief and perspective that I gain when I am able to detach from the constantly turning wheel of events in my life and in the lives of those around me. There will always be a sort of kaleidoscopic series of people, places and situations in my life. Detaching from the hold they produce on my mind does not mean I do not take them seriously. Quite the contrary, when I gain some space, I am more available to myself and others because I am not preoccupied with endless thoughts. When my mind is detached, it is free to go where I call it and be where I choose it to be. There is a serenity that comes over me because I see there is no more point in trying to control events than in trying to control the weather — both will happen the way they will happen.

I am able to release my
tight grip on the day and breathe.

How important is it?

12-Step slogan

The Good-Enough Life

Today I recognize the rich beauty that surrounds me. There is a rhythm and a poetry to life that, though I do not always see it, is always present. I am lucky to be alive. Life is a substance that moves me through it — it surrounds me all the time with its ever-changing yet changeless energy. I feel I cannot love the world enough today. Something in the spirit of life feels benevolent. When I think of the days, months and years I wasted chasing after what I thought was life — trying to create and force into being a scenario that I felt was somehow better than the quiet privilege of being alive, being with life. I am deeply grateful today to know that life is good. I will remind myself of that, and when I forget it — as I will — I will come back to this awareness.

Thank you, life — for being there.

———

What a miserable thing life is; you're living in clover, only the clover isn't good enough.

Bertolt Brecht

Today I see how my dependency on people, places and things began — it was out of loneliness. When I could not connect with people in my home, I came to look to objects to fill me up inside — to be what was missing. It was really just an innocent attempt at being happy. Grabbing on to whatever was available, however desperately, was my only way of trying to feel better — trying to feel less alone. Unfortunately, because things cannot really give or love or touch, and because they ask nothing of me, I came to feel even more alone. I was doubly disappointed — let down first by the people I wanted to believe in and second by the illusion I wanted to believe in.

I forgive myself for my innocence.

———

Only in a house where one has learnt to be lonely, does one have this solicitation for things. One's relation to them, the daily seeing or touching, begins to become love and to lay one open to pain.

Elizabeth Bowen

Someone Else's Process

Today I know that I cannot live closer to another person than I live to myself. There may be years when I am changing rapidly in recovery, and for those I need the support of a program and therapeutic resources. There may be years when others close to me are going through changes that are intense and difficult to live with. I do not have to like this or to be a greater source of support than I am emotionally capable of being, given my own issues and limitations. I have a right to protect myself from someone else's growth process in the same way that I have a right to protect myself from their dysfunctional behavior.

*It gets me nowhere fast
to be too reactive to someone in
the midst of deep change.*

The earth is a beehive; we all enter by the same door but live in different cells.

African proverb

Today I accept that intimacy does not mean living inside another person's skin. Fusion is not closeness. It is an enmeshed state in which neither person clearly experiences themselves. Though it is an unconscious attempt to find one's self in someone else, it is really experienced from within as a loss of self. Rather than decide how I feel on my own, I am essentially waiting to be told how I feel by someone else. It seems less threatening somehow if our feelings match up. It is a comfortable symbiosis, an "us" rather than an "I" in which I feel less worried about being abandoned. I know today that the only person I have any control over is myself. If I choose not to abandon myself, I have my best shot at staying whole and happy.

I am realistic about what
intimacy can and cannot give.

We never touch but at points.
                    Ralph Waldo Emerson

Being Overly Understanding

Today I know that I cannot be understanding about everything. I have limits. Sometimes I use understanding as a defense against experiencing my feelings of anger and fear. As I was growing up, my ability to be compassionate was woefully overtaxed. I operated on overdrive, mistakenly thinking that if I could only be a little more understanding, somehow I would be able to work things out — to make sense out of chaos. Today I see that there would have been far more sanity for me if I had accepted my powerlessness over people, places and things and let go of my compulsion to sort it all out. At least then I might have kept myself. Understanding and compassion are roads to freedom, but when they are abused, they can become their own type of jail.

> *There are some things*
> *that I just can't understand.*

The wretched reflect either too much or too little.

Publilius Syrus

Self-Hatred

Today I will not hate myself for being what I am. Whatever I judge myself to be or I know about myself that I am ashamed of, is not a good enough reason for self-degradation. People tend to treat me the way I treat myself — through my attitude toward myself, I quietly instruct others how to deal with me. Today I see that I am as worthy of decent treatment as they are. It is not my job to make everyone else better before I think of myself or to sacrifice myself to the common good. Once in a while that's fine; as a way of life it doesn't work. It's like trying to drive my car from the backseat. No one likes me for it and I become a backseat driver. The owner of a secondhand life.

I absolutely will not
hate myself today.

———

A man must first despise himself, and then others will despise him.

Meng-tzu

331

What Life Can Give

Today I realize that taking care of myself means different things in different situations — there is no one way to do it and that is why, as a concept, it is so hard to get a hold of. To think that if I do recovery perfectly, do it all just right, I will produce stress-free relationships is magical thinking. It is a repetition of my childhood fantasy that if I just tried a little harder or understood a little better, I could make my family well. When we talk about recovery, we are talking about life and life offers no guarantees. We do what we can do and let go of the results. Recovery is about returning myself to life; it is not about superseding the natural laws of life. I can do only what I can do. My real challenge in life is in expanding the interior of my own soul.

*I ask from life only what it
has the capacity to give.*

———

The nurse of full grown souls is solitude.
James Russell Lowell

Letting Go Of My Smaller Self

Today I walk through my day with self-abandon. So much of recovery tells me to focus on and take care of myself. This is partly for personal and spiritual growth and partly as an antidote for my obsession with others. There is another spiritual truth, however, that one has to lose one's self in order to find one's self — to die to the smaller self in order to be born to the larger self. People who are not preoccupied with their smaller selves seem to have let go of their "inner judgment committee" and released their souls into a freer state of aliveness and being. Today I realize that taking care of myself does not mean getting stuck in my own head. It lies in the paradox of letting go of myself in order to be myself.

I let go of my smaller self
in order to be my larger self.

The individual never asserts himself more than when he forgets himself.

Angelo P. Bertocci

Letting Go Of Problems

Today I allow whatever is troubling me to be turned over. If it is a relationship I cannot sort out, a professional concern I do not know the answer to or a problem that feels insolvable, I will put it in a quiet place, a bubble surrounded with light, and I will let it float upward. Many of the problems that I carry around throughout my day as inner strife I really can do nothing about. When I spend all of my time worrying about them, I have little energy left over for myself and I complicate my day needlessly. Today I will release with love those things over which I am essentially powerless.

I let go of what
I have no control over.

Revenge proves its own executioner.

John Ford

Today I know that self-centeredness is not a correction for co-dependency. When I become as obsessed and preoccupied with the workings of my own mind and personality as I was previously about another person, place or thing, I am essentially developing a co-dependent relationship with myself. The characteristics of co-dependency are delusion, denial and repression. When I am constantly self-occupied and create these characteristics in an intrapsychic relationship with myself, I am co-dependent within me. How can I possibly have anything but co-dependent relationships outside myself if I can't let go within? The only dependency that really works is one on a Higher Power. From there I see more clearly where the rest fits in.

I create a healthy
relationship with myself.

———

Solitude is bearable only with God.

André Gide

Moments Of Enlightenment

*T*oday I see that what is called enlightenment — the holy instant, satori, the awakened state or any such name — is really a very simple experience. It is a feeling of complete openness, a flash of deep awareness, a moment of the direct experience or a sense of oneness. It is a signpost or a brief glimpse of what that higher state of awareness is all about, a moment in which the importance of external objects gives way to a sense of eternal bliss, an awareness that this is not all there is and that life has a deeper meaning. I will welcome these moments of awareness in my day today, reminding me that I am a part of something timeless.

I am glimpsing moments of enlightenment.

Before enlightenment, carry the water, till the soil.
After enlightenment, carry the water, till the soil.

Zen proverb

Today I understand that the thoughts I think and the thought forms that I put out into the ether help to create my future. Much of what I am experiencing today is a result of what I have accepted to be true about myself and my life in the past and the same will be true for my future. I cannot go beyond my own imagination or be someone I cannot first conceive of in my mind. What I hold as possibilities concerning myself are dormant in my subconscious and find a way to my conscious mind in the form of how I feel about myself. I pay attention today to what I put into my own mental computer, knowing that the beliefs that I hold about myself will manifest in my personality, in my relationships and in my life.

I acknowledge the power of my thoughts about myself and my life.

———

My interest is in the future because I am going to spend the rest of my life there.
Charles F. Kettering

337

Blaming Others

Today when I am in a bad mood and feel like blaming someone else for it, I will try something new — I won't. Haven't I got it through my head yet that blaming doesn't work? It makes the other person defensive and deaf to what I say, and it postpones my seeing and understanding what the feeling beneath the blame is. It engages me in a cycle of blame. By the time either of us comes up for air, the battle and the war have been lost and neither of us even remembers what it was about. Today I will recognize that beneath my urge to blame is probably either self-condemnation or a fear of being blamed myself. I will stay with those feelings and see what they are about for me before I act on them by blaming someone else.

*I will connect with my Higher Power
today and see where the connection leads me.*

*It's such a comfort to take the bus
And leave the driving to us.*
Greyhound advertisement

Today I will remember to take care of my-self. This may come in a variety of forms, depending on what stage of life I am in and how I balance my needs. There are, how-ever, things that make me feel especially good. Quiet time to unravel my thoughts and to align myself with a Higher Power is a good activity to make part of my daily schedule. When I let myself get too tired, I feel stressed; when I feel stressed, little things seem big, and when little things seem big, I get short-tempered and do and say things I later regret. I will nurture myself with enough rest and quiet today. I will eat well and take enough time to enjoy my meals, and I will allow myself to relax and enjoy my day.

*I let myself have
the rest and quiet I need.*

———

*HALT — Don't let yourself get too
Hungry — Angry — Lonely — Tired.*

12-Step slogan

Co-creating

Today I nurture my creativity. Creativity is the spontaneous energy that I bring to the tasks of my day. It is an energy that, as it flows through me, nurtures me. My own creativity allows my spirit to flow freely. It is not the result but the act itself. Each time I bring my creative spirit to my way of perceiving something, I co-create what I am seeing. A beautiful day with blue sky, butterflies and birds becomes an experience in which I participate. I actually see myself as being a part of the lovely atmosphere, not only looking on but entering into the experience so that I lose a sense of myself and feel one with the moment.

I co-create my world.

I will not serve that in which I no longer believe whether it calls itself my home, my fatherland or my church: and I will try to express myself in some mode of life or art as freely as I can and as wholly as I can.

James Joyce

My Apology

Today I will apologize to life for all that I have unfairly cursed, judged and, even more seriously, taken for granted. If I am to forgive anyone, I will first have to forgive myself, and in order to do that I sincerely say that I am sorry. I am sorry that in my ignorance I have not understood my power both to hurt or to help another person. I am sorry that there are so many moments of potential beauty that I have let slip by unseen, unnoticed. And I am most particularly sorry that I have not known the difference between love, need and greed, that they have so often masqueraded for each other. I understand now that to have beauty and love in my life, I need to recognize and appreciate it.

I make sincere apologies to life.

Real culture lives by sympathies and admirations, not dislikes and disdains — under all misleading wrappings it pounces utterly upon the human core.

William James

Objects Of The World

Today I realize that accumulating things does not increase my happiness. The objects and activities of the world have only so much to give me and cannot, in and of themselves, bring happiness. As all great religions and philosophies say, happiness lies within. It is the freedom and wisdom with which I move through my life, order my day and look upon the people, places and things close to me that influence the quality of my experience. It is not what I have in my life, but how I feel about what I have that makes the difference. If I own lots of things in such a way that they also own me, I lose my capacity to enjoy them. If, on the other hand, I see them for what they can and cannot give me, I am free to enjoy them.

I see what the things
of the world have to offer.

Man must choose whether to be rich in things or in the freedom to use them.

Ivan Illich

Today I am sure that life operates within certain cosmic laws. What I do that is wrong in the eyes of these laws incurs a sort of debt that some day or another I will have to pay. Willfully doing harm or causing mischief does not go anywhere; my chickens will come home to roost. What I give with sincerity and love will always return to me in some form — it is never a mistake to love. Taking care of myself is a spiritual act and increases my ability to love and be present. I cannot use it to justify self-centered greed and to relieve myself of guilt when I hurt others. Life does not make it clear in the short run, but in the long run there is no free lunch. What I receive, I give, and what I give, I receive.

I respect the natural laws.

———

We have no dues or fees but we do have expenses. Give what you can and if you can't, keep coming back.

Treasurer's announcement
in 12-Step programs

God Is Within

Today I recognize that God is not an idea but an energy, not meant to be thought about but experienced. When I confine my beliefs about God to a locale outside myself, I am giving away the God that lives within me. When I sit quietly and draw to myself the power and energy of a higher force, I am bathing my soul in light — giving my inner being a cleansing bath, removing obstacles from my own path by allowing what I hold in darkness to be exposed to light. When I rest in the knowledge that a Higher Power lives within me, I will always feel access to that energy — this is what the mystics call my own personal God.

*I am aware of the God energy
within and without me.*

———

Be still, and know that I am God.
                                        Psalm 46:10

Today I see all of my addictive behaviors as an attempt to fill a hole that I feel inside of me. The strange thing is that the more I try to fill it with substances such as people, places and things, the bigger it feels. More food, money, sex or intoxicants just create their own need because those things have no power to fill me up. Fullness has to come from within. I experience it as a sense of serenity, inner light or quiet peacefulness. When I use outside substances, even ideas, to deal with my desolation and emptiness, I only keep wanting more. In the case of feeling spiritually full, "less is more." I need to increase my capacity for feeling full, not my capacity for feeling empty.

*I fill up from
the inside.*

Life itself is the proper binge.

Julia Child

Dealing With Negativity

Today when I am bothered by someone else's negativity, I will say a prayer for them. I am not praying for them because I want to be a do-gooder or to show that I am somehow above them. I am praying for them because I see prayer as a dynamic energy and a positive force. Darkness cannot live in light, and negativity cannot grow unless I feed it with more negativity. When I surround the void around someone with light and love, it shrinks; it cannot breathe. The way to cure negativity is not with more negativity. The way to cease hating is not by hating more. Love is restored through the open and free medium of love. It is in this way that I truly protect myself.

*I do not cure negativity by
feeding it with more negativity.*

---

*When thou prayest, enter into thy closet
and when thou has shut the door, pray to thy Father
which is in secret, and thy Father which seest
in secret shall reward thee openly.*

Matthew 6:6

Today I will not insist upon perfection from myself in order to feel good. Why should each thing I do have to be excellent in my eyes or someone else's in order for me to feel happy with it? The idea is that I enjoy the process that what I do feels satisfying and interesting, that I can hold my place in this world with dignity. Being addicted to success every time means that eventually I will dry up my own creative source because success every time is not natural. When I allow myself to enjoy and experience satisfaction with whatever I am doing, I keep the doors open for my own creative flow and a pleasant exchange with others. When I do not accept what I do unless it's just right, I close off my own inner flow.

*I enjoy my
own creative process.*

I think I did pretty well, considering I started out with nothing but a bunch of blank paper.

Steve Martin

Releasing My Need For Perfection

Today I understand that it is my attachment to things and not the things themselves that get me into trouble. An object or person in and of itself does not have the power to enslave me, but the importance I attach to it does. When I want a person, place or thing more than I want a self, I give a part of myself away to that object. It is through my inner heart and soul that I connect with my Higher Power. When my attention is always somewhere else, I considerably reduce my connection with God. This is how my center gets thrown off, and codependency finds a port of entry within my personality. When I maintain my own inner connection with self and Higher Self, I automatically guard against getting lost.

I examine my attachments and how
they operate in my personality.

———

Every form of addiction is bad, no matter whether the narcotic be alcohol or morphine or idealism.

Carl Gustav Jung

Today I recognize that truth is what exists beneath the surface. It is the energy that holds this universe together, the harmony among planets and the order in nature. There is a force that binds life, that is life and that operates at the center of all that is alive. Truth is not what is fabricated, discussed and decided upon as right. It is right itself. When I live in line with truth, my life has a power that does not come from me but flows through me because I place myself at its center. Truth is what cannot be ignored indefinitely. In its vitality I feel life, power and inner direction. Today I bear witness to a deeper reality. I look behind the veil.

Truth is at the
center of my being.

———

Truth exists, only lies have to be invented.
Georges Braque

Giving To Life

Today I am aware that holding back creates a vacuum. If I do not, each and every day, show up for my life and give what I have to give, I cannot really expect to get much back in return. There is a sort of cosmic payroll system that understands how much I am willing to extend myself toward life. If I am generous, it will often give back more than I give in terms of satisfaction and a feeling of being alive in my own skin. If I am stingy, I may feel that life is turning its back on me when actually I am turning my back on life. I will show up for my day today and participate in the life around me.

*I will give to my
life without holding back.*

---

*What you get is living — what you give
is life.*

Lillian Gish

Coming To Terms With Mortality

Today I see that to live life with inner peace one must have an inner awakening. It is imperative that I come to terms with death and my own mortality in order to live with inner freedom. If I see death as a final end, I will carry around a quiet sense of ultimate defeat. Though I may experience a sense of victory remaining alive and healthy, I will see my mortality as something to be conquered rather than befriended. If, on the other hand, I see death as a transition to another state of being, it will appear to me as an extension of life, one which I need not fear. Not an end but a beginning.

*I understand
that life as I know it is
not permanent.*

---

*Death may be the greatest
of all human blessings.*

Socrates

Ownership

Today I see that the spiritual lesson of life is learned in letting go. Ownership of any person, place or thing is an illusion. I own nothing. Even my body is only mine to use; someday it will decay and die like all the things I think are under my control. It was a mistake in my thinking to feel that anyone ever belonged to me. People do not belong to people — no one is meant to live up to my expectations. I am here just to love and accept people as they are. This does not mean that I don't have hopes and dreams for myself and others, only that my love is not contingent upon another person filling my dreams for me.

People belong to themselves
and their Higher Power and so do I.

———

What do you suppose will satisfy the soul,
except to walk free and own no superior?
Walt Whitman

Today I see that when I trust myself, I needn't worry about whether or not I trust others. People in my life will not necessarily be trustworthy every step of the way. If my focus is always on whether or not I can trust others, I will postpone my security and peace of mind indefinitely. It is my own reactions that are important to listen to, understand and act on. When I can trust myself to hear and respond to my own inner voice, then I feel at home and unthreatened in the world. When I wait for others to prove to me that they can be trusted before I will trust myself and act on my own behalf, I give away my power.

> *I have a trusting
> relationship with myself.*

Trust yourself only and another shall not betray thee.

Thomas Fuller

Life Of The Soul

Today I realize that as I grow in recovery and spirituality I am expanding into dimensions of myself that are not common or everyday. I may feel a sense of separateness from types of activities that I used to enjoy. I may experience a growing desire for simplicity and find myself losing interest in situations that now appear not worth the energy I expended on them. Though this may feel lonely at times, I will go beyond that feeling into a new kind of connectedness and belonging. I belong to myself today and I experience great community with my own soul. People need not understand this side of me for me to be comfortable with them. What matters is that I understand it.

I am okay with my
expanding self.

———

He who longs to strengthen his spirit must go beyond obedience and respect. He will continue to honor some laws but he will mostly violate both law and custom.

Constantine Peter Cavofy

Today I see that anxiety arises inside of me when I fear my own inner emptiness. I run from the feeling and try to find activities to keep me from it. I will try something different today. I will accept the emptiness and allow it to be there. Rather than be anxious about it, I will realize that worry will not help it one single bit. I will relax and let the emptiness just be there without running away from it or resisting it. Eventually the feeling will transform into something else and I will allow that to happen. Awareness of a painful state can be all that I need to transform that state into something different. It is in my resisting feeling states that they gain a hold over me — when I allow them to be, they are allowed the room to move and change.

I am aware of my inner states.

———

Courage is resistance to fear, mastery of fear, not absence of fear.

Mark Twain

Changing Others

Today I will lighten up. I notice that I gravitate toward problems and make too much of them. Once I am involved in and focused on a problem, I am loath to let it go. I keep going over it again and again and again. There are so many little things about my life and relationships I can do nothing about. Wouldn't it make my day more pleasant and my insides less tormented if I just accepted this and stopped thinking that I can control and change things? When I put my energy into changing other people, I have none left for my own life.

*I let go of my preoccupation
with other people.*

God grant me the serenity to accept the things I cannot change.

Reinhold Niebuhr,
Serenity Prayer

Today I will not hold myself hostage to my own dysfunctional behavior. I can change. Much of my behavior is composed of habits I learned in childhood. I developed attitudes early in life about who I was and what was possible for me in life. When I carry these habits and attitudes unexamined into my life today, I create a present life that, underneath, looks like my past life. In many ways I would like my life to look different from yesterday. I will take a good, hard look at what I am unconsciously repeating today that I wish to discontinue. I will get the support and help I need to make changes, then I will discipline myself to put those subtle changes of personal behavior into effect.

I can change me.

. . . Courage to change
the things I can. . . .

Reinhold Niebuhr,
Serenity Prayer

What I Can And Cannot Do

Each day I become increasingly clear about the people, places and things in my life over which I have some control and those over which I have none. When I operate under the illusion that I can control what is beyond my ken, I lose my serenity in my frantic efforts to effect change. When, on the other hand, I do not take needed actions to make life changes, I become despondent and discouraged. I let go of that which is essentially beyond my control and I take positive steps to make changes where possible. Today I separate what I can do something about and what I cannot. This is how I retain my peace of mind.

*I see that there
are things I can control
and things I cannot.*

———

. . . *And the wisdom to know the difference.*
Reinhold Niebuhr,
Serenity Prayer

Today I recognize forgiveness as the quickest road to freedom and serenity. When I forgive my past, I release myself from the grip that it has on my present. I no longer carry that heavy baggage around with me. It is difficult to live in peace today if I am psychically engaged in yesterday's battles. Though it may be very painful, I will take on my issues and resolve them to the best of my ability either with the people involved, in a supportive therapeutic situation or within the quiet of my own heart. I cannot forgive and release what I do not first feel and come to terms with. The type of forgiveness that bypasses this stage only pays lip service to letting go. I will do what I need to do today to process fully the parts of my past that remain unresolved so that I can let them go.

I meet my past honestly
and with integrity.

———

Forgive all who have offended you, not for them, but for yourself.

Harriet U. Nelson

Powerlessness Over People

Today I remind myself that the only place from which I can live is inside of me. When I try to live in someone else's insides, I lose my own because I cannot be two places at once. My co-dependency is so second nature to me that I think in terms of other people more quickly than I think in terms of myself. I quietly obsess about how other people affect me, replacing their concerns for mine. What I want (on an almost unconscious level) to change about myself, I attempt to correct in them. The idea that I am powerless over another person is as terrifying to me today as it was as a child, when I could do nothing to help, fix or control my parents. I couldn't then and I can't now.

I accept
my powerlessness
over people.

———

We are all of us calling and calling across the incalculable gulfs which separate us even from our nearest friends.

David Grayson

I Can Learn To Separate

Today I am aware of my fear of being separate. It takes subtle forms because I fear rejection and abandonment. If someone I love disagrees with me or holds a different point of view, I get scared and want either to pull away or to argue until their point of view matches mine. I am aware now that these are separation issues. I was afraid that if I separated from my parents and family, no one would be there when I returned, that things would somehow be changed or different. I did not have the important experience of leaving and returning over and over again, learning that I can be separate and still stay connected. I see now that I need to work on this issue so that I can come to understand that I can have both self and intimate relationships in my life.

I can learn to separate and retain
both myself and another.

———

Self-love, my liege, is not so vile a sin as self-neglecting.

William Shakespeare

361

Time Spent With Me

Today I will remember to stay home and give myself the quiet, comfort and safety of my own company. When I forget how much I need to be with myself, I lose contact with my best friend — me. Any relationship needs time in order to keep it a going concern, and my relationship with myself is no different. Because I spend all of my time housed in my body, I think that I am spending time with myself, but this is not necessarily true. Time truly spent with myself feels different — it has a timeless feeling about it, a quiet meandering quality out of which I become nourished and refreshed. Because it is through my self that I connect to God, eternity or whatever one calls it, time spent with myself is time well spent.

I take time to be with my self.

———

If all your clothes are worn to the same state, it means you go out too much.

F. Scott Fitzgerald

Today I am aware that I have some basic issues — like abandonment. My fear of being left is so powerful and pervasive that I hardly identify it as a fear. It takes so little to activate my feelings of rejection — disinterest from someone I love, a turned away head, those I care about having their own lives and relationships; these things are all frightening to me and have the capacity to mobilize deep feelings of anger, resentment and hurt. I read all sorts of deeper motives into this kind of behavior from other people and create scenarios in my mind where I am ultimately left. I realize today that I cannot have people in my life in a healthy, comfortable way if I am daily haunted by the fear that they will leave me.

I can live a comfortable life.

The first lesson of life is to burn our own smoke; that is, not to inflict on outsiders our personal sorrows and petty morbidness, not to keep thinking of ourselves as exceptional cases.

James Russell Lowell

Balance In My Life

Today I realize that excess in any form does not serve me well. Balance is what brings around a sense of inner security and peace. Even too much recovery has the capacity to throw me out of recovery because health is not so much about what I do but how I do what I do. Activities that I label as positive or nurturing cease to be those things when they get out of control in my life. Part of being a mature adult is that I gain an ability to measure, assess and reflect. It is the freedom and serenity that come with perspective. Because I have greater self-knowledge today, I know how much is too much and when to say not now. I give myself permission to regulate my life in a way that feels good to me, knowing that I gain a greater feeling of serenity from balance than from excess.

I look to achieve balance within.

———

The best things, beyond their measure, cloy.

Homer

Coming Home

Today I know what Dorothy learned in *The Wizard of Oz.* If I ever lose my heart's desire again, I'll never look beyond my own backyard because if it isn't there, I never really lost it to begin with. I understand that recovery is a path back to my own heart, which lay within me, hidden behind my own ignorance. As with Dorothy's journey, it takes courage, brains and feeling to come home. Co-dependency is a result, not a cause. It is a loss of self — a seeking of self everywhere but within me. Recovery is coming home. Even my concept of God calling me is my own internal voice calling me to come home. God and I are one within — we co-habit my heart. When I see God as outside of me or myself as outside of me, I am sowing the seeds of co-dependency.

I am on a road to me.

Stay, stay home, my heart, and rest;
Home-keeping hearts are happiest.
Henry Wadsworth Longfellow

Simplicity

Today whenever I feel lonely, tired or worried, I will not look for what I can add to my day to make it better, but what I can remove. When I quiet myself, my mind expands and lets more in. When it is not fixed on a lot of extra things, my mind has the opportunity to go into a state of rest and renew itself. Life is so full of distractions and temptations to overcontrol and overcommit my time. I will take the time I need to be with myself today. Rather than avoid my innermost self, I will listen. When I relax and sink into time, life feels different. Suddenly what seems important is the contents of the moment, not the contents of the week. I will simplify my day rather than complicate it, knowing that it is in the stillness of the moment that my soul is able to reach out to eternity.

I leave time just to be.

The ability to simplify means to eliminate the unnecessary so that the necessary may speak.

Hans Hofmann

*A*fterword

What Does It Mean To Forgive And Let Go?

Forgiveness and letting go are perhaps among the most difficult steps in the process of recovery. There is something about having problems that makes us feel that we are alive and have a purpose. To forgive and let go — to truly release the held resentment — fill us not only with a sense of freedom but a sense of dread as well — a fear of the void.

If I don't have a problem or painful issue to work on, what will there be of me — without my problems to identify with and occupy my thoughts and emotions, who am I?

Why Do We Forgive?

We forgive, if we are wise, not for the other person, but for ourselves. We forgive, not to erase a wrong, but to relieve the residue of the wrong that is alive within us. We forgive because it is less painful than holding on to resentment. We forgive because without it we condemn ourselves to repeating endlessly the very trauma or situation that hurt us so. We forgive because ultimately it is the smartest action to take on our own behalf. We forgive because it restores to us a sense of inner balance.

What Is Letting Go?

Letting go is the act of forgiveness made manifest. Forgiveness too often gets confused with doing good or with certain kinds of superior behavior. This type of forgiveness is bogus and benefits no one. Letting go is an act of surrender, a recognition and acceptance of things as they are, a coming to grips with the fact that we live in a less than perfect world. It is not just a thought but an actual cellular release, a constant daily process, a turning over.

What Are The Steps On The Way?

There are two very difficult steps or stages on the way to real forgiveness. The first lies in admitting and accepting that there is something to forgive, that life was not what we wished it had been. This requires a working through of the denial and euphoric recall that have sustained us to date. It also implies a willingness to look at and deal with deep issues; to walk the walk and talk the talk.

Another even more difficult step lies in the recognition of when to let go of the past and move on. This kind of maturation and growing up is not something that people from less than functional or adequate pasts find easy to do. Because it is a letting go of the dreams and fantasies that the good parent will come and make things right, it requires true mourning of the lost childhood or parent, an acceptance that what happened happened, and cannot be undone. It is letting go of the dream and giving up the search.

What Part Does A 12-Step Program Play?

In successful 12-Step programs, meetings become the safe family surrogate, and a personal relationship with a Higher Power replaces the internal good parent. Working the 12 Steps provides a sound method to ensure safe passage on the road of self-recovery and discovery, from the surrendering of the self-centered self to the birth into the expanded, spiritual self.

How Does The Process Work?

This process requires a willingness to know one's own truth and the courage and strength to feel pain that has been hidden in silence. Once one comes to embrace this approach, as much as it can hurt, it feels better than acting out or repressing trauma. After past issues become clear and resolved, it takes discipline to maintain new behaviors and perceptions. This is what recovery is all about, a journey toward the light. Carl Jung said that we do not really resolve problems; instead we "climb to the top of a mountain, meditate on them until we see them differently." *A Course In Miracles* calls a miracle a "shift in perception."

When we feel the pain but do not connect with the origin of the pain, when something in our present triggers a past hurt or resentment, it feels as if it is entirely about the present, and the past gets projected onto the present. Problems that are loaded with past issues make the present feel unmanageable.

Energy patterns that store memories can rise to a conscious level, be looked at for what they are, felt and released in what Sigmund Freud called, "making the unconscious conscious."

When Does Forgiveness Happen?

Forgiveness and letting go occur after there is enough personal restoration so that forgiving another no longer compromises the self. In order to rebuild we move through the process of bringing the alienated self back to life and integrating it into the total being. We come to understand that there are other people in the world as well, also with needs and dreams, and that we need to understand and live with them. To forgive and let go are part of coming of age, of taking one's life into one's own hands, of accepting life for what it is and is not, and living it, one day at a time, with choice. A process that occurs over an extended period of time, forgiveness comes when the readiness is there. One day we observe that something that was there is gone and that we are free to move on. Move on.